The Saints' Guide to

LEARNING TO PRAY

The Saints' Guide to
LEARNING TO PRAY

Louise Perrotta

CHARIS

SERVANT PUBLICATIONS
ANN ARBOR, MICHIGAN

Charis Books is an imprint of Servant Publications especially designed to serve
Roman Catholics.

Published by Servant Publications
P.O. Box 8617
Ann Arbor, Michigan 48107

Cover design by Paul Higdon - Minneapolis, Minn.

01 02 03 04 10 9 8 7 6 5 4 3 2 1

Printed in the United States of America
ISBN 1-56955-253-3

To my parents, Roger and Roma Bourassa,
who introduced me both to prayer and to the saints

CONTENTS

INTRODUCTION

A large bookstore near my house hosts weekly discussion groups on topics like writing, investing, travel, and of course, books. A group was in full swing when I walked in one recent evening and found a seat at the coffee bar. Sipping my cappuccino directly across from where a dozen people were having a spirited-looking exchange in American Sign Language, I began fantasizing: If I could gather anyone I chose into a discussion group, who would it be and what would we talk about?

Prayer, I decided in half a heartbeat. And in my mind's eye, I could almost picture my ideal discussion group sitting on folding chairs around the bookstore table. Mary and Joseph would be there. Teresa of Avila, John Chrysostom, Catherine of Siena, Abraham and David, Philip Neri, Francis de Sales, Elizabeth Seton, Mary of Bethany, Thérèse of Lisieux ...

I don't really expect our local Barnes and Noble to be featuring an opportunity like this anytime soon. But while working on this book, I've come to see more clearly that in the Church there already exists an ongoing conversation about prayer, and that we have access to it.

Scripture is our main point of entry, furnishing inexhaustible instruction on prayer and offering countless examples of men and women raising hearts and minds to God in every imaginable life situation. Because the Bible is God's *living* Word, their stories have a unique power to draw us into the dialogue—addressing our hearts, eliciting our response, changing our lives.

God's Word had this effect on the saints, which is why their writings and lives can speak to us even over great divides of time and culture. Though not inspired in the same way as Scripture, the saints' words figure into the great "live" conversation on prayer. Rooted in God's undying Word, these words come from people who are gloriously alive and approachable in the communion of saints.

But if Scripture already contains all we need to know about prayer, why bother to approach the saints? From my own experience, four reasons spring immediately to mind:

—*Variety.* If I hear enough different people speaking about prayer in enough different ways, I just might start to get it.

—*Practical examples.* I'm stimulated by seeing how the saints tried to live out Scripture—especially the parts that aren't spelled out, like how to "pray always" (1 Thes 5:17).

—*Encouragement.* The saints had their weaknesses and their struggles with prayer, just like me. They're credible advisors because they reveal what God can do in ordinary human beings who trust and never leave off talking to him. As Blessed André Bessette used to say, "What the Holy Spirit did for the apostles, he can do for us."

—*Prayer support.* The saints aren't detached observers of my attempts to pray. They're a great "cloud of witnesses" (see Heb 12:1) cheering me on to the goal of union with God, with whom they're now united. On my own journey to God, I find assistance in both what the saints wrote in the past and what they pray for me in the present.

In preparing this book, I've listened in on the saints' discussions with a view to collecting advice about "learning to pray." This is therefore not a guide for scaling the mystical heights. Neither does it cover all types of prayer. Having had to choose just one aspect of a very large reality, I've focused on the personal exchange that takes place when we follow Jesus' command to "go into your room and shut the door and pray to your Father who is in secret" (Mt 6:6).

I've addressed my questions mainly to the men and women whom the Catholic Church officially recognizes as saints or as candidates for canonization. A few members of the discussion are Orthodox saints. Some, like Thomas à Kempis and Brother Lawrence of the Resurrection, are not on the canonization track but produced writings that have led many Christians into lives of prayer.

On the reasonable assumption that you opened this book seeking guidance from the saints and not from me, I have tried to let the saints speak for themselves as much as possible. Except for short chapter introductions, this book consists of their contributions, roughly arranged according to subject.

Look through the table of contents, dip into the book here and there, or read chapter by chapter, according to your inclination. Linger over whatever catches your attention. Perhaps you'll find a thought to mull over or a saintly friendship to pursue. Ask your own questions about prayer, and know that what you'll find here is the tiniest sampling of what the saints have to say on the subject. Think of this book as a mere chip from the richest of diamond mines, and be inspired to go digging for yourself!

As I compiled this book, I thought often of an image suggested by a fourteenth-century Dominican mystic named Henry Suso. Whenever he was assailed by thoughts of his unworthiness, he imagined himself a beggar positioned outside the door of a banquet hall where God was dining with his closest friends. As the privileged diners emerged, Henry saw himself addressing them, "so that I might receive some small savor of their sweet fullness." Whenever he received so much as a word in return, said Henry, he was "as joyful as though I had found a treasure. I held it to me tenderly and said: 'Ah, sweet Lord, how I desire thee. Shall I ever be able to say: Thou art mine and I am thine'?"

And this, I suggest, is the spirit in which we should approach this book. Let's allow its words of saintly advice to lead us beyond conversation *about* prayer and deeper into that great conversation with God which is prayer itself.

ONE

EVERYONE'S INVITED

We love," Scripture says, because God "first loved us" (1 Jn 4:19). That's also why we pray—because God's love melts our chill, sparks our desire, ignites our love. The saints exemplify what happens to people who respond whole-heartedly to these divine initiatives: they are transformed, as sparks of love leap up into a great blaze of union with God.

Fortunately for those of us who are better described in terms of smoldering wicks or flickering flames, many saints wrote of their prayer life in a way that can encourage our own. One is the sixteenth-century Spanish Carmelite Teresa of Avila. Personable, practical, and profound, Teresa is a credible guide for spiritual strugglers because, by her own admission, she dabbled in prayer for almost two decades until a religious awakening prodded her on. Often during those years as a mediocre nun, she confides, "I was more occupied in wishing my hour of prayer were over, and in listening whenever the clock struck, than in thinking of things that were good."

To Teresa's astonishment, God didn't give up on her but kept calling gently. Once she got the message, he led Teresa to the heights of mystical prayer. *God is calling you, too,* is her confident message to us. "Who can possibly despair, when he put up with *me* for so long?"

Teresa is hardly condoning delay or halfheartedness. Divine calls require serious responses. Certainly, "there is no one for whom God makes it impossible to buy his riches," she says of the fruits of prayer. But "if you are to gain this, he would have you keep back nothing." And note this disarmingly simple but arduous piece of advice: "All that the beginner in prayer has to do ... is to labor and be resolute and prepare himself with all possible diligence to bring his will into conformity with the will of God."

Calls and responses, commitments and resolutions—the following selections from Teresa and other saints touch on aspects of this dynamic of prayer. Never mechanical, it is at the very heart of intimacy with a loving God who, Teresa asserts from experience, never fails to repay anyone who turns to him. "For mental prayer is nothing else, in my opinion, but being on terms of friendship with God, frequently conversing in secret with him who we know loves us."

Awakenings of Love and Desire

All through our life Christ is calling us. He called us first in baptism, but afterwards also; whether we obey his voice or not, he graciously calls us still.... He calls us on from grace to grace, and from holiness to holiness, while life is given us....

It would be well if we understood this. But we are slow to master the great truth, that Christ is, as it were, walking among us, and by his hand, or eye, or voice, bidding us to follow him. We do not understand that his call is a thing which takes place now. We think it took place in the apostles' days, but we do not believe in it, we do not look out for it in our own case. We do not have eyes to see the Lord.

John Henry Newman

This Lord of ours is so anxious that we should desire him and strive after his companionship that he calls us ceaselessly, time after time, to approach him; and this voice of his is so sweet.... His appeals come through the conversations of good people, or from sermons, or through the reading of good books ... through sicknesses and trials, or by means of truths which God teaches us at times when we are engaged in prayer; however feeble such prayers may be, God values them highly.

St. Teresa of Avila

We are not drawn to God by iron chains, like bulls and wild oxen. We are drawn by enticements, sweet attractions, and holy inspirations.... Grace is so gracious, and so graciously seizes our hearts to draw them ... that our free will suffers no violence.... How gently God handles our hearts! How skillfully he imparts his strength without interfering with our freedom.... He adjusts his power to his gentleness in such a way that when it comes to doing good, his might gives us power, while his gentleness maintains our freedom of will.

St. Francis de Sales

Our good God waits for us patiently in our delays, he unceasingly calls us even though we don't answer him; he knocks at the very door of the heart which is shut to him....

When we feel urged to depart from a sin, to leave an imperfection, to correct a negligence, to grow in virtue, to make rapid strides to the perfection of divine love, then the hour is come for us. Let us arise in haste, let us run to the divine Spouse, accept his grace, benefit by his inspiration; it is the hour of our deliverance; let us not delay, let us run!

St. Jane Frances de Chantal

Anyone who has not begun to pray, I beg, for love of the Lord, not to miss so great a blessing. There is no place here for fear, but only desire.

St. Teresa of Avila

Oh, eternal wisdom! ... How skillfully you play the game of love; how well you can adapt yourself to the one you desire! Who else would woo his beloved as long as you do? Who would wait as patiently? Who else would remain as constant, in face of so many rebuffs, as you do, gentle, faithful, adorable Lord and Spouse of all loving souls? And because of all this, my own soul leans towards you, for you are the Good which—through its essential goodness—draws to itself all the ends of the earth.

Up, my children, the time has come!... Open the door, unlock your heart, let your lover enter, make up for the long time you have wasted by giving yourself to him in tender, devoted love.

Blessed Henry Suso

Christ doesn't play favorites, he told St. Catherine of Siena, "but I do respect holy desire." To Venerable Charles de Foucauld he said: "Prayer is primarily thinking of me with love—the more anyone loves me, the more he prays. Prayer is the attention of the soul lovingly fixed on me. The more loving that attention is, the better is the prayer."

Dorothy Day was in a common-law marriage, pregnant, Communist, and searching for God when she noted these stirrings of prayer in a 1925 diary entry:

I am surprised that I am beginning to pray daily. I began because I had to. I just found myself praying. I can't get down on my knees, but I can pray while I am walking. If I get down on my knees I think, "Do I really believe? Whom am I praying to?" And a terrible doubt comes over me, and a sense of shame, and I wonder if I am praying because I am lonely, because I am unhappy.

But when I am walking up to the village for the mail, I find myself praying again, holding the rosary in my pocket that Mary Gordon gave me in New Orleans two years ago. Maybe I don't say it right but I keep saying it because it makes me happy....

Then I think suddenly, scornfully, "Here you are in a stupor of content. You are biological. Like a cow. Prayer with you is like the opiate of the people....

"But," I reason with myself, "I am praying because I am happy, not because I am unhappy...."

And encouraged that I am praying because I want to thank him, I go on praying. No matter how dull the day, how long the walk seems, if I feel low at the beginning of the walk, the words I have been saying have insinuated themselves into my heart before I have done, so that on the trip back I neither pray nor think but am filled with exultation.

Choosing and Persevering

You will become holy if you desire it.

Blessed Marie of the Incarnation

Let us remember that God ... has chosen never to put force upon our will. Let this be deeply impressed upon your heart: God in his love for us has desired to save us by his Son, but our salvation is not his will unless it is ours also.

St. Louise de Marillac

St. Teresa of Avila called prayer "the royal road to heaven" and stressed the importance of a good, resolute start for anyone who wants to travel it to the end.

How shall they begin? The most important thing, indeed, *the* important thing is for them to have a strong and resolute determination not to stop until they reach the sources of the living water.... They are determined to go forward, no matter what happens, despite all obstacles, all difficulties, all slander. They must say to themselves: I will keep going whether I reach the end of the journey or whether I die on the way, even if I do not have the courage to endure the difficulties I meet with, even if the world sinks under me! Often we are warned: "there is danger in that path"; "so-and-so was lost here"; "that person went astray"; "this one who prayed so much fell"....

Pay no attention to the fears they may suggest to you or to the dangers they describe.... Do not let yourselves be deceived by anyone: there is but one road [to the fountain of living water] ... and that is prayer.

He who perseveres to the end shall be saved. Piety must be habitual, not by fits. It must be persevering, because temptations continue all our life, and perseverance alone obtains the crown. Its means are the presence of God, good reading, prayer, the sacraments, good resolutions often renewed, the remembrance of our last ends.

St. Elizabeth Ann Seton

Dogged prayer reaches its goal. And if at the beginning prayer seems to you dry and stony, still from this hardest of rocks you will squeeze the oil of grace if only you persevere, if protracted delay does not sap your strength, if your longings do not grow slack from deferral. Deferral is obviously painful to a lover but desires prolonged grow stronger.

Gilbert of Hoyland

In your spiritual ascent and your search for a closer union with God, you must allow yourself no rest, no slipping back. You must go forward till you have obtained the object of your desires. Follow the example of mountain climbers. If your desires turn aside after objects that pass below, you will lose yourself in byways and your mind will be drawn in all directions. Your progress will be uncertain. You will not reach your goal. And you will not find rest after your labors.

But if your heart and mind, led by love and desire, withdraw from the distractions of the world, you will grow strong. Your recollection will deepen the higher you rise on the wings of knowledge and desire. Little by little as you abandon baser things to rest in the one true and unchangeable Good, you will dwell there, held fast by the bonds of love.

St. Albert the Great

Choices Made Concrete

The saints made practical resolutions about how to express and pursue their decision for Christ in their daily lives. Without slavishly imitating their lists, we can do the same. Solanus Casey jotted down these simple themes in 1897, shortly after he entered the Capuchin seminary. They became an integral part of his approach to God.

Means for Acquiring the Love of God

I.   Detachment of oneself from earthly affections. Singleness of purpose!

II. Meditation on the Passion of Jesus Christ.

III. Uniformity of will with the Divine Will.

IV. Mental prayer—meditation and contemplation.

V.   Prayer—"Ask and it shall be given to you" (Mt 7:7).

The same year, while on retreat in Nazareth, Venerable Charles de Foucauld noted some resolutions in the form of instructions given him by Christ:

"Pay unceasing attention to me, and devote as long as possible to interior prayer and sacred reading, for they will make you one with me and through them I shall speak to you as I used to speak to my parents at Nazareth.... Base yourself on me. Lose yourself in me, immerse yourself in my love....

"Never miss a possible moment, an instant, in the presence of the Blessed Sacrament.... The whole universe is nothing beside the Master of the universe who dwells in the tabernacle."

Dorothy Day, a woman noted for her active promotion of social justice, made these resolutions to keep her focused on God in the midst of her busy life.

— "Can you not watch one hour with me?" (see Mk 14:37). I shall remember this whenever I am tired and want to omit prayer, the extra prayers I shall set myself....

— Morning prayers, in my room before going to Mass. I always omit them, rushing out of the house just in time as I do. If I were less slothful it would be better....

— Around the middle of the day to take, even though it be to snatch, fifteen minutes of absolute quiet, thinking about God and talking to God.

— Read the Office as much as I can....

— One visit [to the Blessed Sacrament] during the day, always without fail.

— Rosary daily.

— I do plenty of spiritual reading to refresh myself and to encourage myself so I do not have to remind myself of that.

— The thing to remember is not to read so much or talk so much about God, but to talk to God.

— To practice the presence of God.

— To be gentle and charitable in thought, word, and deed. (Most important of all.)

Elisabeth Leseur, married to a loving but militantly atheistic doctor, made these practical decisions in 1911:

To fast: spiritually, by more constant efforts with myself and sacrifices and suffering; physically, by self-denial in food, by privations and all my bodily misery. [Sick all her life with hepatitis, Elisabeth was diagnosed with cancer in 1911.]

To pray: by confession, more fervent Communions, meditation on the Passion, visits to the Blessed Sacrament, the rosary, the penitential psalms, the Way of the Cross; by sermons and pious exercises, by more constant and peaceful union of my soul with God.

Almsgiving: Of a little money, but also of my time, my heart, my prayers, and my suffering. To have a boundless charity in my heart—sweet, tender, strong, always active and including everyone, especially people who don't attract me.

To become humbler, more silent about myself....Not to look dejected, not to carry human dissatisfactions as if they were a heavy burden, but to let my joy shine on all, the fruit of renunciation and penance.

Reflect on the everlasting love God has had for you.... He has always loved you from all eternity, and for this reason he has prepared for you all these graces and favors.... Among other things, he has thought of enabling you to make your resolutions to serve him....

Beloved resolutions, you are the fair tree of life that God with his own hand has planted in my heart, the tree my Savior desires to water with his blood to make them fruitful!... Fair and holy resolutions, if I keep you, you will keep me. If you live in my soul, my soul will live in you.

Live then forever, resolutions which are everlasting in the mercy of my God! Live eternally in me, and let me never forsake you!

St. Francis de Sales

TWO

A FEW GOOD HABITS

If you are careful to form habits of the kind I have mentioned, you will derive such great profit from them that I could not describe it even if I wished." The voice is St. Teresa of Avila's; the "habits" are basic disciplines of prayer—things like showing up regularly and focusing. Each in their own way, all the saints cultivated these disciplines, establishing habits and priorities that served as openings to grace.

St. Edith Stein (Teresa Benedicta of the Cross in religious life), who converted to Catholicism in 1921 after reading St. Teresa's autobiography, took the Carmelite mystic's advice seriously. Edith discovered the benefits of healthy routine early in life. She was raised in a devout Jewish home where religious customs and traditions were faithfully observed. A disciplined scholar, she developed into an outstanding philosopher. In 1933 she entered the Carmelites, embracing a structured prayer life that included daily Mass, the Divine Office, and two hours of meditation. The Nazis disrupted this in August 1942 when they arrested Edith and her sister Rosa. The two women were taken to Auschwitz and gassed.

For more than ten years before her entry into religious life, Edith was a brilliant lay professional who taught, wrote, and lectured widely. From experience, she knew how challenging it can be to balance daily commitments and give God priority. This is why, in a 1932 lecture, she insisted on each Christian's responsibility to select some prayer practices and shape them into a flexible "plan for daily and yearly living ... in order to make ready the way of the Lord."

As a concrete suggestion, Edith offered the following approach for beginning a busy day. Like the best saints' advice on prayer, it is practical and realistic.

The duties and cares of the day ahead crowd about us when we awake in the morning.... Now arises the uneasy question: How can all this be accommodated in one day? When will I do this, when that?... Agitated, we would like to run around and rush forth. We must then take the reins in hand and say, "Take it easy!... My first morning's hour belongs to the Lord...."

So I will go to the altar of God [to Mass].... And when the Lord comes to me then in Holy Communion, then I may ask him, "Lord, what do you want of me?" And after quiet dialogue, I will go to that which I see as my next duty.

Make Room for God

The biggest challenge many of us face in our prayer lives is finding time and a quiet place to hear God. The saints dealt with this too. They encourage us to make quiet time with God our top priority.

A little sprinkling of water which merely settles the dust and dampens the surface is useless for enriching the soil; plenty of water is needed.... In the same way, we need an abundance of heavenly dew and water if we are to bring forth the fruit of good works. With good reason, then, we are advised to take as much time for prayer as we can.... Often enough, it takes us half an hour just to quiet our mind and tune our instrument, so to speak....

But whoever is pressed for time on account of many duties should keep offering his little coin, like the poor widow in the temple. If no negligence is involved, God, who provides for all created things according to their needs and nature, will provide for this need too.

St. Peter of Alcantara

We ought to have fixed times for prayer.

St. Jerome

If you avoid unnecessary talk and aimless visits, listening to news and gossip, you will find plenty of suitable time to spend in meditation on holy things.

Thomas à Kempis

We should find a quiet place where we can go alone for our time of prayer. Our Lord said, "Whenever you pray, go into your room and shut the door and pray to your Father who is in secret" (Mt 6:6)....

Jesus Christ especially delights in meditations made before the Blessed Sacrament and gives most abundant light and grace to those who visit him there.... In our world, it isn't just anyone who receives permission to speak alone with a king. But everyone can speak with Jesus, the King of Kings, whenever they wish. Rich or poor, upper-class or lower-class—people of all kinds can come before the Blessed Sacrament to express their desires and seek his grace. There Jesus gives audience to all, listens to all, comforts all.

St. Alphonsus Liguori

Prayer's Daily Rhythms

St. Vincent de Paul gave this advice to some Sisters of Charity in 1640. It's helpful for anyone who wants to start the day with God.

Rise punctually.... The whole order of the day depends on this first action. You must acquire this habit courageously.... Our bodies are like donkeys—accustomed to one road, they will always follow it. To make this habit easy, make it a rule to go to bed at the right time....

Always do what you can to make prayer your first occupation so that your mind may be filled with God for the rest of the day.

In his Introduction to the Devout Life, *St. Francis de Sales gives a four-point instruction on beginning each day.*

1. Thank and adore God wholeheartedly for the blessing of having been kept alive by him during the night. If you fell into any sin in the course of it, ask his forgiveness.

2. Realize that the present day has been given you so that

through it you may win the coming day of eternity. Make a firm resolution to use the day well for this purpose.

3. Think ahead to the work, contacts, and other opportunities for serving God that you might encounter during the day. Foresee which temptations might arise to lead you into sin, whether through anger, pride, or some other lack of self-control. Prepare yourself by making a holy resolution to use well all the means you will be offered to serve God and advance in devotion; likewise, resolve to avoid, fight, and conquer whatever might arise to oppose your salvation and God's glory....

4. Humble yourself before God, acknowledging that by yourself you can carry out none of your plans.... As if you were holding your heart in your hands, offer it to God with all its good intentions. Implore him to take it into his protection and strengthen it for success in his service.... Ask Our Lady, your guardian angel, and the saints to help you in all this.

Our morning offering ... seals the whole day.... If it is made fully and sincerely—even though we should forget to renew it from hour to hour as we commonly do, and not retract it by any act of our will—and if no mortal sin comes in the way, our first good offering secures all we do for the day. What a comfort that is!

St. Elizabeth Ann Seton

During the activities of the day, ... unite your will to God's by confirming your morning resolution. Do this either by a simple, loving glance at God, or by a few words spoken quietly.... "Yes, Lord, I want to do this action because you want it," or simply, "Yes, Father," or, "O Holy Will, live and rule in me," or other words that the Holy Spirit will suggest to you. You may also make a simple sign of the cross over your heart.... All this will show that above everything, you want to do the holy will of God and seek nothing but his glory in all that you do.

St. Jane Frances de Chantal

St. Edith Stein recommended breaking up a busy workday with "breathing spaces" for turning to the Lord.

Each one must know, or get to know, where and how she can find peace. The best way, when possible, is to shed all cares again for a short time before the tabernacle.... And when no outer rest whatever is attainable, when there is no place in which to retreat, if pressing duties prohibit a quiet hour, then at least she must for a moment seal off herself inwardly against all other things and take refuge in the Lord. He is indeed there and can give us in a single moment what we need.

"By the morning exercise, you open the windows of your soul to the Sun of Justice. By the evening exercise, you close them to the darkness of hell," says St. Francis de Sales. A pre-bedtime "examination of conscience" is indispensable. "Everyone knows how it should be done," he says, then spells it out anyway:

1. We thank God for having protected us during the day.
2. We examine how we behaved in the course of the day. To make this easier, we think about where we were, with whom, and what we were doing.

3. If we find that we did something good, we thank God for it. On the other hand, if we discover that we sinned in thought, word, or deed, we ask God's forgiveness, resolving to mention this in confession at the earliest opportunity and to diligently change our ways.

4. We then entrust to Providence our body and soul, the Church, relatives, and friends. We ask Our Lady, our guardian angel, and the saints to watch over us and for us. With God's blessing, we go to take the rest he ordained that we need.

Special Prayer Times and Seasons

While prayer is a daily encounter with God, the saints also recognized particular seasons, days, even moments, of his grace.

Sunday is the property of our good God; it is his own day, the Lord's day. He made all the days of the week. He might have kept them all. He has given you six and has reserved only the seventh for himself.

St. John Vianney

St. Bernadette saw the moments after receiving Holy Communion as a most precious time of prayer. "How do you manage to remain so long at your thanksgiving?" a nun asked her one day.

Bernadette replied, "I think to myself that the Blessed Virgin is giving me the Infant Jesus. I welcome him, I speak to him, and he speaks to me."

The Catholic liturgy has a great charm for me. I love to

live, in the course of the year, the great collective life of the Church, uniting myself with its joys and sorrows, joining my feeble prayers with its prayers, my weak voice with its strong voice. It is sweet to me to go through the liturgical cycle, reliving our Savior's life, his incarnation and death and ascension; through the mouths of the prophets, fathers, and saints of all ages to tell him my faith and my love; to adore him in company with those who have adored him through the centuries; to offer myself to him with shepherds, disciples, martyrs, people of all times; to feel myself a living link in the great Catholic union; and following after so many people and preceding so many others, to come with my homage to the infant God, the suffering Christ, the risen Lord.

Elisabeth Leseur

Sometimes the liturgical cycle—or the cycle of events in one's own life—is occasion for taking a spiritual retreat.

Servants of God ought to set aside a fixed time in which to devote themselves to prayer. In addition to this ordinary and daily exercise, they should at times withdraw completely from every kind of occupation, however holy, in order to concentrate on spiritual exercises.... This may be done at any time, but especially for the principal feasts of the year, in periods of trouble and distress, or after a long journey or any absorbing business which may have led to distraction and dissipation of heart.

St. Peter of Alcantara

A retreat is to the whole of life what meditation is to a day. The soul gathers new strength and resumes the daily duty changed and sanctified. Giving myself is easier when my soul has been replenished.

Elisabeth Leseur

The Discipline of Solitude

It is spiritual solitude that the Lord Christ requires of you, though bodily withdrawal is not without its uses when it may be had, especially in time of prayer. You have his own commandment in the matter: "When you pray, enter into your room...." (Mt 6:6). He himself practiced what he preached: he would spend all night in prayer, not only hiding from the crowds but not allowing even his closest friends to come with him.... You must do likewise when you want to pray.

Be quite clear that the only solitude required of you is that of mind and spirit. You are alone in spirit if you are not thinking about ordinary matters, if you are not interested in things present, if you reject worldly values, if you keep out of quarrels, if you do not resent injuries or hug grievances. Otherwise you are not really alone, even when you are alone in body. Do you see that it is possible both to be alone in a crowd and to be in a crowd when you are alone? No matter how many people there may be around you, you are alone, if only you do not pry eagerly into their conversation or judge it harshly.

St. Bernard of Clairvaux

Silence is the great master. It speaks to the human heart. Silence is not an empty void; God dwells therein.

Père Jacques (Lucien-Louis Bunel)

St. Thomas More took to heart the contrast between Jesus, who often spent his nights in prayer, and the "hypocritical Pharisee," who spent his nights comfortably in bed.

How I wish that those of us who are prevented by our own laziness from imitating the illustrious example of our Savior might at least be willing to call to mind his all-night vigils when we turn over on the other side in our beds, half asleep, and that we might then, during the short time before we fall asleep again, offer him thanks, condemn our slothfulness, and pray for an increase of grace. Surely if we set out to make a habit of doing even the least little bit of good, I feel certain that God will set us forward a great way on the path of virtue.

Blessed are the nights which God allows me to spend in intimate conversation with him. My Lord and my God, let me realize the value of such moments as much as I should.... Teach me to extend those hours where I keep solitary vigil at your feet while the world slumbers....

Our Lady of Perpetual Help, I have never prayed to you in vain.... Keep your hand on me to prevent me from sleeping at Jesus' feet, as I unfortunately do so often when he invites me to pray to him and with him, to spend an hour alone with him.

Venerable Charles de Foucauld

Just Do It!

What wife is there who would not give her husband at least a ring ... as a mark of her love and an assurance that she will be his until death? Does our Lord, then, deserve less, that we should mock him by giving and then taking back the trifle we gave him? But this little bit of time we decide to give him out of all the time we spend on ourselves and on others, ... let us give ... with a firm determination never to take it back, [considering it] as something that no longer belongs to us.

St. Teresa of Avila

Let us confess our shortcomings to God and on no account abandon diligence in prayer. For it is better to be blamed for frequent omissions than for complete neglect.

St. Mark the Ascetic

THREE

A QUESTION OF ATTITUDE

In prayer, as in the rest of life, it's possible to spoil a good thing by approaching it with the wrong attitude. Spiritual writers over the centuries have therefore stressed the importance of coming to prayer with the right spirit—among other things, with humility, faith, reverence, and love.

Blessed Columba Marmion gave a simple explanation of these foundational attitudes by contrasting two scriptural figures who illustrate opposing approaches. On one side is the "praying" Pharisee of Jesus' parable, who proudly calls God's attention to his supposed superiority and great achievements: "I fast twice a week; I give a tenth of all my income" (Lk 18:12). "God detests such self-righteous people, though they may be very correct and irreproachable," Abbot Marmion observed.

On the other side is St. Paul, who refused to pride himself on his accomplishments. His attitude was "I see my own righteousness as rubbish. My confidence is in Jesus, who alone gives value to what I do" (see Phil 3:4-11; 2 Cor 11:30; 12:9). St. Paul took pride in his weaknesses and not in his works, said Marmion. People like him are "dear to God because they glorify his Son."

Confidence in God and clear-sighted humility—while these attitudes characterize every saint's prayer life, they are especially obvious in that of St. Thérèse of Lisieux, who made them the centerpiece of her "little way" to holiness. She called not for great works but for doing life's ordinary tasks with great love and joyful trust. Her way, said St. Thérèse, was like "an elevator to carry me to Jesus, for I was too small to climb the steep stairs of perfection." Meditating on Jesus' welcome of little children, Thérèse rejoiced in her littleness. To her mind, it was a positive advantage, proof of her claim on God's mercy: "It is your arms, Jesus, which are the elevator to carry me to heaven." Becoming great is not the goal here. "In fact, just the opposite: I must become less and less."

Each in his or her own way, Columba Marmion, Thérèse, and all the saints encourage us to ground our prayer in the self-knowledge that leads to true humility and hope in God. These are the attitudes explored in this chapter. Essentially, they revolve around two questions: Who is God? Who am I?

The saints' answers to these two questions drew them into intimacy with God. We might ask ourselves: Where are our answers drawing us?

The Great Discrepancy

St. Catherine of Siena's confessor described the following experience as "the solid foundation for Catherine's life of union with Christ" and said it contained a truth "of depth unfathomable."

Our Lord appeared to Catherine while she was meditating and said: "Know, my daughter, who you are and who I am. If you learn these two things, you will be truly blessed. You are she who is not, and I AM he who is. If your soul becomes deeply penetrated by this truth, the enemy can never deceive you, and you will avoid all his snares. You will never agree to do anything against my commandments, and you will easily acquire grace, truth, and peace."

Blessed Raymond of Capua

Spying on St. Francis of Assisi at prayer one moonlit night, his friend Brother Leo saw him lying face up, arms outstretched in a cross, repeating over and over: "My dearest Lord and God, what are you? And what am I, your little useless worm of a servant?" Later, asked for an explanation, Francis said: "In that prayer you heard, two lights were manifested to me: one light in which I knew the Creator, and one in which I knew myself.... I saw the infinite depth of the divine Godhead and my own wretched abyss of misery. And so I said, 'What are you, Lord, the highest, the wise, the all-good, the all-merciful, that you trouble yourself about me...?'"

Try this exercise to get an idea of just how stupid it is to ignore the gap between God's greatness and your sinfulness, suggests St. Thomas More. Picture yourself as a criminal guilty of high treason. You're headed for execution when the prince, who is inclined to mercy, gives you an audience with him—a chance for freedom, if only you demonstrate a change of heart. Now, imagine yourself throwing that chance away by taking a careless, cavalier approach to the meeting.

While he stays in one place and listens attentively, stroll around here and there as you run through your plea. Then, when you have had enough of walking up and down, sit down on a chair, or if courtesy seems to require that you condescend to kneel down, first command someone to come and place a cushion beneath your knees.... Then yawn, stretch, sneeze, spit without giving it a thought, and belch up the fumes of your gluttony. In short, conduct yourself in such a way that he can clearly see ... that while you are addressing him you are thinking about something else....

Certainly we would consider it quite mad to defend ourselves in this way before a mortal prince.... And do we think it is reasonable ... to beg pardon so contemptuously from the King of all kings...?

God loves the humble, while he resists the proud. If we elevate ourselves through pride, God will withdraw from us and we will fall into dense darkness. If we are humble, he will approach us, console us, hear our prayers, and send us away justified.

St. Frances Cabrini

On March 24, 1620, as Blessed Marie of the Incarnation was walking to work and praying about her business affairs, she had a mystical insight into God's love and her own sinfulness that changed her forever.

In a flash the eyes of my mind were opened and all the faults, sins, imperfections I had ever committed were represented to me both in general and in particular, with a distinction and clarity more certain than any certitude that human effort could produce.... At the same moment I saw myself completely immersed in blood, and I was convinced that it was the blood of the Son of God ... and that this precious blood had been shed for my salvation.

If the goodness of God had not sustained me, I believe I would have died of fright, so horrible and shocking is the sight of sin, however small it may be. No human tongue can express it.... To see a God-made-man die to expiate sin ... and in this way reconcile sinners to him!...

In this same moment my heart felt snatched from itself and transformed into his love, ... and the experience of this love begot in me the most intense sorrow and regret for having offended him....

I returned to our home changed into another person, but so powerfully changed that I didn't know myself anymore. I saw unmasked my ignorance which had caused me to believe that I was quite perfect, that my actions were innocent, and finally that all was well with me; but now I humbly confessed that my justices were but iniquities.

The Glory in Weakness

We must always live in the knowledge that we can do nothing by our own strength. We will then be imitating St. Philip Neri, who used to say to God every morning upon awakening, "Lord, keep your hand over Philip today, for if not, Philip will betray you."

This is all the grand science of Christians: to know that we are nothing and can do nothing of ourselves.... Then we will never neglect to seek through prayer that strength which we do not have on our own and which we need in order to resist temptation and do good. And so with the help of God, who never refuses anything to those who pray to him in humility, we will be able to do all things.

St. Alphonsus Liguori

If you were at the point of death, what thought would give you confidence about standing before God's judgment seat to give an account of your life? Here's what St. Claude la Colombière said would help him:

It would be nothing other than the number and greatness of my sins. Here is a confidence really worthy of God: far from allowing us to be depressed by the sight of our faults, it strengthens us ... by its infinite conception of the goodness of our Creator.

Our imperfections should not please us, ... but on the other hand they should not dismay or discourage us. We should rather make them a cause for submission, humility, and being on our guard against self; but not for discouragement or affliction of heart, and even less for a lack of confidence in God's love for us; for though it is true that God does not love our imperfections and venial sins, he loves us very much in spite of them. Thus a child's weakness and infirmity does not please a mother but she nevertheless goes on loving her child, even tenderly and with compassion....

Live joyfully. Our Lord's eyes are on you and he is looking at you lovingly, all the more tenderly because you are so helpless. Never allow your will to foster contrary thoughts; and when they beset you, do not look at them in themselves, turn your eyes away from their iniquity, and turn towards God with brave humility, speaking to him about his ineffable goodness which makes him love our poor, feeble, and abject human nature in spite of its infirmities.

St. Francis de Sales

Always turn your eyes from the study of your own sin to the contemplation of God's mercy. Devote much more thought to the grandeur of his love for you than to your unworthiness towards him, to his strength than to your weakness. When you have done this, surrender yourself into God's arms in the hope that he will make you what he requires you to be and that he will bless all you do.

St. Vincent de Paul

Fr. Solanus Casey, writing to a woman who had asked his spiritual counsel:

Your failure, yes, is an indication of weakness of some kind, somewhere. But if "the weak thing[s] of this world hath God chosen to confound the strong...," as St. Paul so wonderfully assures us ... [1 Cor 1:27], then why ever be discouraged...?

Why, dear sister, you ought to rather thank God for having given you such an opportunity to humble yourself and such a wonderful chance to foster humility—and by thanking him ahead of time for whatever crosses he may deign to caress you with, [having] CONFIDENCE in his wisdom. Confidence in God—the very soul of prayer— hardly comes to any poor sinner like we all are without trials and humiliations.... There is a little verse I am sure will profit you to keep in mind and ought [to] help you foster confidence in God: *"God condescends to use our powers if we don't spoil his plans by ours."* God's plans are always for the best, always wonderful. But most especially for the patient and the humble who trust in him are his plans unfathomably holy and sublime.

Thérèse is weak, very weak. Every day she has a new and healthy experience of this reality. But Jesus takes pleasure in teaching her how to "glory in her weakness" (2 Cor 11:5). This is a great grace; in it we find peace and tranquillity. When we see ourselves so needy, we no longer wish to look at ourselves but only at the Beloved.

St. Thérèse of Lisieux

My God, speak to me of hope....

You forbid me ever to become discouraged at the sight of my shortcomings or to tell myself: "I can't go any further. The road to heaven is too narrow...."

You forbid me to look at my faults—those faults for which I ask your forgiveness every day and into which I fall back endlessly....

You forbid me to look at the infinite graces you have showered on me and at the unworthiness of my present life and to tell myself: "I haven't made good use of so many graces. I should be a saint, and I'm a sinner. After all God has done, there's nothing good in me. I'll never get to heaven." You want me to hope in spite of everything.

Heaven and me, this perfection and my wretched state—whatever can these things have in common?

Your heart, my Lord Jesus. Your heart creates the link between two things that are so unlike.

Venerable Charles de Foucauld

Don't be ever scrutinizing your poor little heart in fear, but look at him. He possesses for you ... all that your poverty lacks.

Blessed Columba Marmion

What Is Needed Is Trust

Written during a time of great personal distress and darkness, this meditation is a classic expression of trusting confidence in God.

God has created me to do him some definite service. He has committed some work to me which he has not committed to another. I have my mission. I may never know it in this life, but I shall be told it in the next. Somehow, I am necessary for his purposes.... God has not created me for nothing. I shall do good. I shall do his work. I shall be an angel of peace, a preacher of truth in my own place, ... if only I keep his commandments and serve him in my calling.

Therefore, I will trust him.... He does nothing in vain. He may prolong my life, he may shorten it; he knows what he is about. He may take away my friends, he may throw me among strangers, he may make me feel desolate, make my spirits sink, hide the future from me. Still, he knows what he is about.

John Henry Newman

Then I saw truly that it gives more praise to God and more delight if we pray steadfast in love, trusting his goodness, clinging to him by grace, than if we ask for everything our thoughts can name.... The best prayer is to rest in the goodness of God.

Julian of Norwich

Dorothy Day received many letters in response to her columns in The Catholic Worker *newspaper—among them "so many sorrowful letters," whose writers she reminded "to pray for consolation, healing, light, courage, strength to endure."*

Prayers are always answered (one way or another). Such prayers bring strange joy on occasion, even in the midst of seemingly unmitigated grief, even despair. Even in the midst of horror, one suddenly feels the touch of God's hand and knows with Julian of Norwich that somehow or other "all will be well"—that "the worst has already happened and been repaired."

Imprisoned by the Nazis before being deported to a death camp, Blessed Titus Brandsma maintained trusting confidence in God and wrote in his journal that he felt "secure and happy" in prison. On the wall of his cell, he pinned a prayer he had discovered as a boy in his grandfather's prayer book; it had sustained him all his life:

Let nothing disturb you, nothing frighten you.
All things are passing.
God alone is unchanging.
Patience gains all.
The person who has God wants for nothing.
God alone suffices.

St. Teresa of Avila

Prayer and faith united are unimaginably powerful. If the saints worked wonders and prodigies, they did it through prayer with faith.... Always pray with Jesus, remembering that a person united with Jesus can do everything. Keep this verse in mind: "I can do all things in Christ who strengthens me" (Phil 4:13). Have faith, pray with faith, and good and overflowing measure will be given you.

Faith, beautiful daughter of Heaven, come live in us!

St. Frances Cabrini

FOUR

BUT WHAT DO YOU SAY?

J ust speak to God from the heart," the saints advise us. "Prayer
should be like a pleasant confidence between father and child,
or between friend and friend," St. John Vianney told his parish-
ioners. "Nothing could be more simple."

Those of us who often feel tongue-tied when we go to pray
can take heart in noticing that while the saints did simply speak
to God, they also used formal prayers. First and foremost, they
used and reflected on the prayer that Jesus taught us, the Our
Father. They turned to the psalms, as Jesus himself did during
his earthly life (see Mk 14:26 and 15:34). Many prayed the
rosary, as well as other traditional prayers.

Whether formal or spontaneous, their prayers fell into the
basic types that are normative for all Christian prayer: adoration
and praise, thanksgiving, confession of sin, petition and intercession. As you'll see in this chapter, the saints offer many helpful insights into each of these modes.

St. Francis of Assisi had a great love for the Our Father,
encouraged his brothers in Christ to pray it often, and wrote a
prayer paraphrasing it. He loved the psalms and arranged various
psalm verses into a number of original prayers. Devotion to
Christ's passion led him to write a short "prayer of the cross" for
recitation when visiting a church. But we especially remember

St. Francis for his spontaneous praise of God in creation.

"Even toward little worms he glowed with a very great love," wrote his biographer and contemporary, Thomas of Celano. No matter how lowly the creatures, Francis "used to praise in public the perfection of their works and the excellence of their skill, for the glory of God."

Francis' best-known prayer of praise is probably his "Canticle of the Sun." Though composed when Francis was dying and almost blind, it is joyfully exultant. Read and pray its first stanzas, and perhaps you'll be inspired to continue in your own words!

Most high, omnipotent, good Lord,
Yours are the praises, the glory, the honor, and all blessing.
To you alone, Most High, do they belong,
And no one is worthy to speak of you.

Praised be you, my Lord, with all your creatures,
Especially honored Brother Sun,
who makes the day and illumines us through you.
And he is beautiful and radiates with great splendor
And bears your likeness, Most High One.

Praise and Adore

What a gift prayer is! It is the real treasure of our soul, our being able to give to God the worship of perfect adoration.

St. Frances Cabrini

This blessed moment of outdoor prayer took place in 1789, when St. Elizabeth Ann Seton was fifteen.

I set off to the woods about a mile from home and soon found an outlet to a meadow, and a chestnut tree attracted my attention, and when I came to it I found rich moss at the foot. There then was a soft seat; the sun was warm, the air still, a clear blue vault above; and all around I heard the numberless sounds of the joy and melody of spring. The sweet clover and wild flowers I had gathered by the way were in my hand. I was filled with love of God and admiration, enthusiastic even, of his works....

God was my Father, my all. I prayed, sang hymns, cried, laughed, talking to myself of how far he could place me above all sorrow. There I lay still to enjoy the heavenly peace that came over my soul, and I am sure, I grew, in the two hours so passed, ten years in my spiritual life.

If only we could say in utter truth these words, "My God is my all," we would never find our prayer long or boring. When boredom descended upon us in prayer, that simple phrase said from the heart would act like a spell to drive away our weariness and disgust.

St. Jane Frances de Chantal

Ask Forgiveness and Mercy

I come to your feet, most loving Father. Behold, my sins have made a separation between you and me. Ah! Have mercy on me according to the multitude of your mercy, break down the wall of my old way of life which keeps me from you; and draw me so vehemently toward you that I may, in the gentleness of your inextinguishable cherishing-love, wisely follow you by loving.

Loving-kind Jesus, although the will to do what is good is in me, I do not find the strength to accomplish it. Therefore ... turn my soul from the frailty of the human condition toward you in such a way that I may untiringly run in the way of your commandments and cling inseparably to you.

St. Gertrude the Great

You are here in me, my God.

And before you, in you, morning to evening, at every moment,

I commit imperfections, sins without number in thought, word, and deed.

I'm terrified. I feel like saying, "Depart from me, Lord, for I am a sinner."

But I don't say it.

No, on the contrary:

"Stay with us, Lord, for night is falling."

I am in the night of sin, and the light of salvation cannot come to me except through you.

Stay, Lord, for I am a sinner.

Venerable Charles de Foucauld

Give Thanks

Let us thank God at all times and under whatever circumstances. Thank him for our creation and our existence. Thank him for everything—for his plans in the past that by our sins and our want of appreciation and patience have so often been frustrated and that he so often found necessary to change. Let us thank him for all his plans for the future—for trials and humiliations as well as for great joy and consolations; for sickness and whatever death he may deign to plan.

Therefore we should thank him frequently for not only the blessings of the past and present, but thank him ahead of time for whatever he foresees is pleasing to him that we suffer.

Solanus Casey

Know that gratitude for God's benefits is one of the riches of the soul, and that ingratitude dries up the fountain of divine graces. Give your tribute of gratitude often to the most loving Jesus. Often look back over your lives and consider the graces, both general and particular, that you have received. If you meditate well, you will perceive the torrents of these saving waters of divine grace which have poured into your soul at the various stages and circumstances of your lives.

With how much care our dear Jesus has always watched over you! How admirably he guided you into the way of eternal salvation! God has worked many wonders for you because he loves you well. But remember that all he has done for you up to now is but a slight pledge of his great love for you. If you are faithful in his holy service, he will work wonders in you.

St. Frances Cabrini

"In all things give thanks to God" (1 Thes 5:18)—but do so in a way that honors him, warns St. Bernard of Clairvaux, for "even the Pharisee gives thanks" (see Lk 18:11).

Do you not perceive that the Pharisee, in offering thanks, honors God with his lips but in his heart pays tribute to himself? And so, through force of habit more than by intention or inclination, you will hear people of all sorts pronouncing words of thanks, for even the wickedest persons will offer a perfunctory thanks to God ... when their perverse will is fulfilled. For instance, when the thief has bagged the loot for which he has planned, he celebrates in the privacy of his hideout and says: "Thank God! I have not watched in vain, the night's work has not been wasted." The murderer will brag and express his thanks for the overthrow of a rival, for having had revenge on an enemy. And the adulterer will utter an irreverent "Thank you, God" as he capers with delight on having gone to bed at last with the woman he has long pursued.

It is clear then that God will listen only to the thanks that spring from a pure and genuine simplicity of heart.

Ask and Intercede

John Damascene says that "to pray is to ask fitting things of God." It often happens that our prayers are not granted because we ask for that which is not good for us: "You ask and do not receive, because you ask wrongly" (Jas 4:3).

It is no easy matter to know what we should pray for, since it is difficult to know what we ought to desire.... For this reason the apostle Paul says that "we do not know how to pray as we ought" (Rom 8:26).

Now Christ is our teacher.... Therefore, his disciples said to him, "Lord, teach us to pray" (Lk 11:1). It follows, then, that we pray most rightly when we ask for what he taught us to pray for. Consequently, Augustine says, "If we would pray rightly and fittingly, we should say nothing else but what is contained in this prayer of our Lord."

St. Thomas Aquinas

I can state quite briefly what you ought to pray for: Pray for a happy life.... Perhaps you ask, "What is a happy life?" ... The person who is truly happy is the one who has all that he wishes to have, and wishes to have nothing which he ought not to wish.

St. Augustine

St. Catherine of Siena's great spiritual work, The Dialogue, opens with a third-person reference to herself as "a soul" who presents the Father with four requests—only one of them for herself.

A soul rises up, restless with tremendous desire for God's honor and the salvation of souls....

Now this soul's will was to know and follow truth more courageously. So she addressed four petitions to the most high and eternal Father, holding up her desire for herself first of all—for she knew that she could be of no service to her neighbors in teaching or example or prayer without first doing herself the service of attaining and possessing virtue....

The second was for the reform of holy Church. The third was for the whole world in general.... In her fourth petition she asked Divine Providence to supply ... for a certain case [perhaps a criminal awaiting execution, or a priest struggling with despair.]

Simple Words

You don't need to use many or high-sounding words. Just repeat often, "Lord, show me your mercy as you know best." Or, "God, come to my assistance."

Macarius the Great

St. Peter Julian Eymard, who founded two religious orders dedicated to the Eucharist and to adoration of the Blessed Sacrament, suggested these conversation topics for a Holy Hour with Jesus.

Speak to him of himself, of his heavenly Father, of all that he has done for his Father's glory; this will gladden his heart. Speak to him of his love for men and women; this will fill his heart and yours with happiness. Speak to him of his mother, and you will be praising his filial affection. Speak to him of all the saints; this will glorify his divine grace in them.

Jesus ... will then speak to you about yourself. Under the influence of this conversation, your heart will be filled with peace and joy.... In silence and rest you will hear Jesus' gentle voice penetrating your soul. Not only that— your very silence and stillness will be transformed into the highest activity of love: *You will become one with him.*

What most hinders the action of grace in our souls is the

fact that we are no sooner in our good Master's presence than we immediately expand on our troubles and sins. This wearies our minds and weighs down our hearts with sorrow.... To avoid this danger, we should begin by expressing our joy: "Dear Lord, it's a pleasure for me to visit you. I'm happy to spend this short hour with you. How good of you to call me here! How good of you to love me as you do! From now on, I will love you intensely in return."

Then, in spirit, enter into the heart of Jesus to love and adore.

You wrote to me: "To pray is to talk with God. But about what?" About what? About him, and yourself: joys, sorrows, successes and failures, great ambitions, daily worries—even your weakness! And acts of thanksgiving and petitions—and love and reparation.

In short, to get to know him and to get to know yourself—"to get acquainted."

Blessed Josemaría Escrivá de Balaguer

—Let your prayer be completely simple, for both the publican and the prodigal son were reconciled to God by a single phrase....

—Let there be no studied elegance in the words of your prayers. How often the simple and monotonous lispings of little children make their fathers give in to them....

—Do not launch out into long discussions that fritter away your mind in efforts for eloquence.... A single word full of faith saved the good thief.

St. John Climacus

However quietly we speak, he is so near that he will hear us: we need no wings to go in search of him but have only to find a place where we can be alone and look upon him present within us. Nor need we feel strange in the presence of so kind a Guest; we must talk to him very humbly, as we should to our father, asking him for things we should ask a father, tell him our troubles, beg him to put them right, and yet realize that we are not worthy to be called his children.

St. Teresa of Avila

... And Sometimes No Words

For me, prayer is a surge of the heart, a simple glance toward heaven, a cry of gratitude and love in the midst of trial as well as joy.

St. Thérèse of Lisieux

You have undoubtedly experienced in your own life a deep, legitimate affection for your father or mother, sister or brother, when nothing is said. At that moment a simple look or handshake says it all; the entire heart is moved. The best in oneself goes out to meet the best in another, who experiences this deep affection. Those moments and those very simple expressions of love between God and ourselves are the essence of prayer.

Père Jacques (Lucien-Louis Bunel)

When you feel invited to remain in silence at our Lord's feet like Magdalene, just *looking at him with your heart*, without saying anything, don't cast about for any thoughts or reasonings, but just remain in loving adoration.

Blessed Columba Marmion

During one time of prayer, Blessed Marie of the Incarnation found herself unable to express to God her great longing for him.
Thus I said to him: "You understand, O Love, you understand." Then words failed me completely and I remained in this silence.

FIVE

THE BOOK THAT COMES ALIVE

If personal prayer is an opportunity for encountering God, it makes sense to go into it Bible in hand. No prayer book compares with God's Word, which not only inspires our listening and speaking to God but communicates his presence. As Vatican II put it: "In the sacred books the Father who is in heaven comes lovingly to meet his children, and talks with them.... Prayer should accompany the reading of sacred Scripture, so that a dialogue takes place between God and man" ("Dogmatic Constitution on Divine Revelation," paragraphs 21, 25).

The saints pursued this dialogue by praying with the Bible, especially the Psalms and the Gospels. Some saints also dedicated themselves to Scripture study so as to make the whole Bible more accessible to others.

The great fourth-century scholar St. Jerome undertook to provide not just commentaries but an accurate Latin Bible. The massive project took twenty-two years, not counting time spent mastering Greek, Latin, and—"with much toil and effort"— even Hebrew. Driving his scholarly efforts was the conviction that "ignorance of the Scriptures is ignorance of Christ" and that Christians need guides who can show them "Jesus concealed beneath the letter."

St. Jerome came to Scripture study via a frightening dream in which he saw himself before the heavenly judgment seat.

"Whose disciple are you?" the Judge asked.

"Christ's," Jerome answered.

"You're lying," replied the Judge. "You're Cicero's disciple, not Christ's."

Afterward, a shaken Jerome admitted that his addiction to the elegant writing of pagan authors like Cicero had left him unable to open the Bible without shuddering at what he considered its uncouth style. Deeply repentant, he threw himself into biblical studies, communicating his findings through personal instruction as well as writing, especially in the monastic communities he founded in Bethlehem. Some of his disciples, among them St. Paula and St. Marcella, themselves became knowledgeable guides to Scripture.

Any honest biography of St. Jerome reveals him as a perplexing mix of scholarship, piety, and irascibility. "Patron saint of grouches," a friend of mine calls him. At the same time, Jerome is admirable for his austerities, compassion for the poor, and zeal to meet Jesus in his Word.

Because my husband and I often write about the Bible, we have gotten into the habit of praying nightly to St. Jerome. As you reflect on the place of Scripture in your own life, you might want to invoke him too.

St. Jerome, pray for us.

Approaching the Bible

Anyone who thirsts for God eagerly studies and meditates on the inspired Word, knowing that there he is certain to find the one for whom he thirsts.

St. Bernard of Clairvaux

A number of saints left prayers that we can use as we sit down to read Scripture. This one, which focuses on the Gospel accounts of Christ's suffering and death, is from St. Thomas More.

Good Lord, give us your grace not to read or hear this Gospel of your bitter Passion with our eyes and ears in the manner of a pastime. But may it, with compassion, so sink into our hearts that it may serve for the everlasting profit of our souls.

All sacred Scriptures should be read in the spirit in which they were written. In them, therefore, we should seek food for our souls rather than subtleties of speech.... Curiosity often hinders us in the reading of the Scriptures, for we try to examine and dispute over matters that we should pass over and accept in simplicity. If you desire to profit, read with humility, simplicity, and faith.

Thomas à Kempis

Friends of St. Dominic left this description of how he interacted with God's Word.

He would sit quietly, and after the sign of the cross, begin to read.... His spirit would then be sweetly aroused as if he heard Our Lord speaking.... As if disputing with a companion he would first appear somewhat impatient in his thought and words. At the next moment he would become a quiet listener, then again seem to discuss and contend. He seemed almost to laugh and weep at the same time, and then, attentively and submissively, would murmur to himself and strike his breast....

Dominic used to venerate the book, bow to it, and kiss it.... Following this, ... he would reverently rise and incline his head for a short time. Wholly refreshed and in great interior peace, he then returned to his book.

The Word That Speaks

Our meditations on the Word who is the Bridegroom, on his glory, his elegance, power, and majesty, become in a sense his way of speaking to us.... When with eager minds we examine his rulings, the decrees from his own mouth; when we meditate on his law day and night, let us be assured that the Bridegroom is present, and that he speaks his message of happiness to us.

St. Bernard of Clairvaux

Tested by illness and spiritual darkness, St. Thérèse of Lisieux was feeling "a bit sad" one evening toward the end of her life. Is God "really pleased with me?" she wondered, and wished someone could tell her. Just then she was handed a note from her older sister, a Carmelite nun in the same convent.

"You told me that you were pleased with everything about me, that I was especially cherished by God," Thérèse told her sister later—but she was unconvinced: "Always the thought that your love made you see what wasn't there prevented me from rejoicing fully." It took a confirming word from Scripture to show Thérèse that her sister had written the truth.

I took my little book of the Gospels, asking God to comfort me, to answer me himself.... And it so happened that my glance fell on this passage that I had never noticed before: "He whom God has sent speaks the words of God, for he gives the Spirit without measure" (Jn 3:34). Oh, then I cried tears of joy!... It's you, my little Mother, whom God has sent for me. You're the one who brought me up, who caused me to enter Carmel. All the great graces of my life I have received through you. You speak the same words as God, and I do believe now that God is very happy with me, since you tell me so.

St. Jerome gave this advice about Scripture reading to a young Roman woman named Eustochium in 384. Both she and her mother, Paula, are honored as saints.

Read often, learn all that you can. Let sleep overcome you, the book still in your hands; when your head falls, let it be on the sacred page.... Keep close to the footsteps of Christ, and, intent on his words, say, "Did not our hearts burn within us on the road while Jesus opened the Scriptures to us?" (Lk 24:32).... Do you pray? You speak to the Bridegroom. Do you read? He speaks to you.

The farther I go into the Gospels and epistles, the more I find grace, strength, and incomparable life. God is indeed there. Every day I come away from this reading more satisfied and strengthened. My will is reinforced there, my heart warmed. Through this Book of books, God the Supreme Teacher educates my inmost being, helping me to understand life, to smile at duty, and to will more strongly.

Elisabeth Leseur

Praying With Scripture

John Cassian's account of the advice given him by an Egyptian monk named Abba Isaac presents the spirit of lectio divina— *prayerful focusing on a Scripture text through reading, listening, and communing with God.*

To keep the thought of God always in your mind you must cling totally to this formula for piety: "Come to my help, O God. Lord, hurry to my rescue" (see Ps 70:1).

This verse ... bears all the feelings that human nature can experience. It can be adapted to every condition and deployed against every temptation. It carries a cry to God in the face of every danger. It piously confesses humility. It conveys our sense of frailty, our assurance of being heard, our confidence in help that is always and everywhere present. Someone forever calling out to his protector is very sure of his nearness.

This short verse is an indomitable wall for all those struggling against the onslaught of demons. Whatever the disgust, the anguish, or the gloom in our thoughts, it keeps us from despairing of our salvation since it reveals to us the One to whom we call, the One who sees our struggles and who is never far from those who pray to him.

If things go well for us in spirit, this verse is a warning. We must not get puffed up at being in a good condition that we cannot retain without the protection of God for whose continuous and speedy help it prays. This little verse, I am saying, proves to be necessary and useful to each one of us in all circumstances.

St. Teresa of Avila drew on her Gospel reading as an aid to personal prayer.

I would try to picture Christ as within me, [dwelling on] those times of his life when he was most lonely. It seemed to me that his being alone and afflicted, like a person in trouble, allowed me to approach him more easily. I had many simple thoughts of this kind. I used to find myself most at home during Christ's prayer in the Garden, where I would go to keep him company. I thought of the bloody sweat and of the affliction he endured there. Had it been possible, I would have liked to wipe that painful sweat from his face.... I used to remain with him there for as long as my thoughts allowed....

For many years, nearly every night before I fell asleep, ... I used to think a little of this prayer in the Garden.... I believe that my soul gained very much in this way, because I began to practice prayer without knowing what it was.

Many Scripture verses make good prayers. Dorothy Day suggested using these three to ask for faith, hope, and charity:

"Lord, I believe, help my unbelief" (Mk 9:24).

"In you I have hoped; let me never be put to shame" (see Ps 25:2; 31:14, 17).

"Dear Lord, take away my 'heart of stone' and give me a 'heart of flesh,' so I may learn to love, to grow in love" (see Ez 11:19).

A classic way to pray with Scripture is to put yourself in the place of various biblical figures—and not only the admirable ones!

I am the lost sheep and you are the Good Shepherd.... I

am, alas! the Prodigal Son who wasted your substance, your natural and supernatural gifts, and reduced myself to the most miserable state because I had fled far from you.... What more can I say? I am the treacherous disciple who betrayed you, the presumptuous man who disowned you, the coward who mocked and derided you, the cruel wretch who crowned you with thorns. I scourged you, I laid the cross upon you, I mocked you in your agony, I buffeted you, I gave you gall and vinegar to drink, and it was I, alas! who pierced your heart with the cruel lance. All this and even more I have done with my sins! What a thought to make me humble!

Blessed Pope John XXIII

The Bible's Book of Prayers: the Psalms

Elizabeth Seton loved and prayed the psalms all her life. In 1803, as her husband, William, lay dying of tuberculosis while in quarantine at an Italian port, she kept their spirits up by reading the psalms aloud.

"Often when he hears me repeat the psalms of triumph in God," she wrote, "it so enlivens his spirit that he also makes them his own, and all our sorrows are turned into joy."

After William's death, Elizabeth experienced a "sad weariness" and hard soul-searching about whether to leave the Episcopal Church: "So painful and sorrowful an impression is left on my heart, it is all clouded and troubled," she wrote a friend. "So I say the penitential psalms, if not with the spirit of the royal prophet [David], at least with his tears.... Yet with such confidence in God that it seems to me he was never so perfectly my Father and my All at any moment of my life before."

An exultant psalm—the first verse of Psalm 68—expressed Elizabeth's sense of joy at receiving her first Communion as a Catholic: When Jesus entered "the poor little dwelling so all his own, the first thought I remember was, let God arise, let his enemies be scattered, for it seemed to me my king had come to take his throne."

> If the psalm prays, you pray too. If it laments, do the same. If it gives thanks, rejoice along with it. If it speaks in the accents of fear, tremble with it. For all that is written in the psalms is meant to be a mirror for us.
>
> *St. Augustine*

Blessed Marie of the Incarnation experienced and recommended the psalms as "spiritual food" that "continually fills the soul with loving thoughts of God."

In the psalms I saw God's justice, his judgments, his grandeur, his love, his equity, his beauties, his magnificence, his generosity.... I saw that the goodness of this divine spirit had established me in green and fertile pastures which kept my soul so nourished that it overflowed and I could not keep silent....

This took me so completely out of myself that as I went about the monastery I was in a constant state of ecstasy. It was the same while I was at work. Sometimes my thoughts were concentrated on the purity of God and how all things declare his glory. The psalm "the heavens declare the glory of God" (Ps 19) had an attraction for me which pierced my heart and enraptured my spirit. "Yes, yes, O my Love! 'Your testimonies are true; they are justified of themselves.

They give witness to the foolish' (Ps 19:8). Send me over the whole world to teach those who are ignorant of you!"

I am easily cast down by suffering and would be inconsolable about my sickness if I did not find in the psalms those cries of sorrow ... which God at last answers by granting pardon and peace. During many weeks of extreme fatigue, the psalms have never been out of my hands. I have not wearied of rereading those sublime lamentations, those flights of hope, those entreaties full of love which correspond to all the wants and miseries of human nature.... Though the psalms were composed long ago, we still find in them the expression of our deepest anguish and the consolation of our sorrows.

Blessed Frederic Ozanam

Take and Read

I'm always encouraging you—and I'm not going to stop encouraging you!—to keep on reading sacred Scripture. And don't let anyone say to me silly, contemptible words such as "I'm stuck at the courthouse all day." "I'm tied up with political affairs." "I'm in an apprenticeship program." "I've got a wife." "I'm raising kids." "I'm responsible for a household." "I'm a businessman. Reading the Bible isn't my thing."

What are you saying, man? It's not your business to pay attention to the Bible because you're distracted by thousands of concerns? Then Bible reading belongs *especially* to you. You're always standing in the line of battle, you're constantly being hit, so you need *more* medicine than other people. For not only does your wife irritate you, but your son annoys you, and a servant makes you lose your temper. An enemy schemes against you, a friend envies you, a neighbor insults you, a colleague trips you up. Often a lawsuit impends, poverty distresses, loss of possessions brings sorrow. At one moment success puffs you up; at another, failure deflates you. How many powerful inducements to anger and anxiety, to discouragement and grief, to vanity and loss of sense, surround us on every side! A thousand missiles rain down from every direction. And so we constantly need the whole range of equipment supplied by Scripture.

St. John Chrysostom

St. Ephrem's sheer delight on reading the Book of Genesis holds out a promise of good things to come as we immerse ourselves in Scripture.
I read the opening of this book and was filled with joy,
for its verses and lines spread out their arms to welcome me;
the first rushed out and kissed me,
and led me on to its companion;
and when I reached that verse wherein is written the story of Paradise,
it lifted me up and transported me from the bosom of the book
to the very bosom of Paradise....

Scripture brought me to the gate of Paradise.

SIX

WHAT TO DO WITH YOUR MIND

Prayer is "nothing other than a raising of the mind to heavenly things," said St. Francis de Sales, quoting many earlier spiritual writers.

"Yes, but you don't know *my* mind," some of us might retort.

"I try to pray, but my thoughts are all over the place."

"Most days, my mind is going a mile a minute. I feel too agitated for prayer."

"I'd pray better if I could just turn my mind off or make it blank."

If you've ever considered your mental processes a hindrance to holiness, you'll be interested in the saints' wisdom about how to make your mind an ally for prayer. Familiar with the same inner resistances we experience, the saints learned to use their thinking, willing, and imagining in turning to God. Some of them explored and explained the role of the mind in relation to various types of prayer—vocal, mental, contemplative. Outstanding among these spiritual guides is St. Francis de Sales.

Named bishop of Geneva in 1602, as the Catholic Church was struggling with the effects of the Reformation, Francis focused on renewing his diocese by leading people to deeper intimacy with God. Given his insistence that holiness is for everyone, along with his genius for teaching the ways of prayer,

Francis is someone we can still seek advice from today. We can find it in his published letters of spiritual direction, in notes taken from his sermons and talks, and in his books. Read part two of his classic *Introduction to the Devout Life*, for example, and you'll come away with many insights into "what to do with your mind" when you go to pray.

As St. Francis points out, our minds themselves are changed as we bend them to prayer: "Since prayer places our intellect in the brilliance of God's light and exposes our will to the warmth of his heavenly love, nothing else so effectively purifies our intellect of ignorance and our will of depraved affections." Centuries before Francis, a saint named Paul touched on a similar point: "Do not be conformed to this world," he urges us, "but be transformed by the renewing of your minds" (Rom 12:2).

Even Saintly Minds Need Help

Anyone whose mind has wandered at Mass will relate to St. Anthony Mary Claret's description of the distracted prayer he often experienced during his three years as a factory worker in Barcelona, Spain. Counsel from a wise priest finally helped him out of his difficulty.

My only goal and all my anxieties were about manufacturing. I can't overstate it—my obsession approached delirium....

It is true that I loved to think and dwell on my projects, but during the Mass and my other devotions I did not want to and I tried to put them out of my mind. I told myself that I'd think about them later but that for the present I only wanted to think about what I was doing and pray. My efforts seemed useless, like trying to bring a swiftly rotating wheel to a sudden stop. I was tormented during Mass with new ideas, discoveries, etc. There seemed to be more machines in my head than saints on the altar....

It happens that the soul will be in the greatest quiet and the intellect will be so distracted that it won't seem that the quiet is present in the intellect's house.... Perhaps it's only my intellect that's like this, and others' intellects are not.... Sometimes I want to die in that I cannot cure this wandering of the intellect.

St. Teresa of Avila

Although our outward aspect is appropriate to prayer, for we kneel and appear to those who see us to be praying, in our thought we imagine something pleasant, graciously talk with friends, angrily abuse enemies, feast with guests, build houses for our relatives, plant trees, travel, trade ... consenting to any thought that comes along.

St. Nilus of Sinai

Blessed Pope John XXIII wrote in his journal on Friday, August 24, 1900:
That blessed rosary went rather badly again this evening. And yet, I am sure I do not do this on purpose; every now and then, as soon as I notice my thoughts are straying, I do try to concentrate.

My God, how far I am from acting according to what I know so well! I confess it: my heart goes after shadows. I love anything better than communion with you. I am ever eager to get away from you. Often I find it difficult even to say my prayers. There is hardly any amusement I would not rather take up than set myself to think of you. Give me grace, O my Father, to be utterly ashamed of my own reluctance! Rouse me from sloth and coldness and make me desire you with my whole heart. Teach me to love meditation, sacred reading, and prayer. Teach me to love that which will engage my mind for all eternity.

John Henry Newman

No Mindless Repetitions!

I do not say mental rather than vocal prayer: to be prayer at all, it must be with reflection. For although the lips may be very busy, I do not call that prayer in which we do not consider with whom we are speaking, nor what we are praying for, nor whom we are to pray.... Anyone who has the habit of speaking to his Majesty as he would to his slave, not noticing if he speaks poorly, but who says just what comes into his head or what he has learned by heart for repetition, to my mind does not pray. Please God, may no Christian act in this manner.

St. Teresa of Avila

To mutter something with the lips is not praying if one's heart is not joined to it.

St. Francis de Sales

Coming Into God's Presence

The practice of the presence of God is an application of our mind to God, or a remembrance of God present, that can be brought about either by the imagination or the understanding.

Brother Lawrence of the Resurrection

Since we're praying to the Creator of the universe, says St. Vincent de Paul, it's "only reasonable" to prepare by asking ourselves questions like these:

How are we going to behave? Before whom are we to appear? What are we going to say? What is the grace for which we ought to ask? It very often happens that carelessness and sloth intervene, or hurry and confusion of mind prevent reflection, so that we fail in preparation. This is a fault that must be checked.

St. Francis de Sales suggests four ways of placing ourselves in God's presence before we pray. "Don't try to use them all together, but only one at a time, briefly and simply."

The *first* consists in an alert, attentive awareness of God's presence everywhere—that is, that God is in all things and all places and that there is nothing and nowhere in this world where he isn't truly present....

The *second* way to place yourself in this holy presence is to reflect that God is present not only in the place where you are but very specially in your heart and in the center of your spirit, to which he gives life and vitality by his divine presence. He is present there as the heart of your heart and the spirit of your spirit....

The *third* way is to think of our Savior, who in his human form sees from heaven all the people in the world—particularly Christians, who are his children, and even more especially those who are praying and whose actions and behavior he notices. This isn't just imagining.... As St. Stephen was being martyred, this is how he saw God (Acts 7:55)....

The *fourth* way consists in using our imagination to picture the Savior in his sacred humanity as if he were near us, just as we sometimes picture our friends present....

Prayer consists in turning the mind to God. Do you wish to know how to turn your mind toward God? Follow my words. When you pray gather up your whole self, enter with your Beloved into the chamber of your heart, and there remain alone with him, forgetting all exterior concerns; and so rise aloft with all your love and all your mind, your affections, your desires, and devotion.

And let not your mind wander away from your prayer, but rise again and again in the fervor of your piety until you enter into the place of the wonderful tabernacle, even the house of God. There your heart will be delighted at the sight of your Beloved, and you will taste and see how good the Lord is, and how great is his goodness.

St. Bonaventure

Just Imagine ...

St. Jane Frances de Chantal described three ways of praying and advised people to pursue whichever one attracted them most. The first is a matter of "using our imagination" to explore a mystery—here, the Nativity:

We picture Jesus in the manger, between an ox and a donkey, in the arms of his holy mother and of great St. Joseph. We look on as his mother places him in the crib, then picks him up to nurse him—to nurse this Son who is her Creator and God.

But don't get fixated on trying to see all these things too specifically, wanting to imagine what this holy infant's eyes look like and how his mouth is shaped. The point is to portray the mystery very simply for ourselves.... This way of meditating is good for people whose minds are filled with worldly concerns. If their imaginations are fully engaged when they pray, all other thoughts will be put to flight.

Among the types of prayer proposed by St. Ignatius of Loyola is the "application of the senses." In spirit, with the imagination, the person praying applies each of the five senses successively to subjects such as scenes from Christ's life. Here is the basic approach:

The first point is to see the persons in my imagination, contemplating and meditating in detail [on] the circumstances surrounding them, and I will then draw some spiritual profit from this scene.

The second point is to hear what they are saying, or what they might say, and I will reflect within myself to draw some fruit from what I have heard.

The third point is to smell and taste in my imagination the infinite fragrance and sweetness of the Divinity, and of the soul, and of its virtues, and of all else, according to the character of the person I am contemplating. And I will reflect within myself to draw spiritual profit therefrom.

The fourth point is to use in imagination the sense of touch, for example, by embracing and kissing the place where the persons walk or sit, always endeavoring to draw some spiritual fruit from this.

You can use your imagination to explore different aspects of your relationship with God.

I began to live as if only God and I existed in the world. Sometimes I considered myself before him as a miserable criminal at his judge's feet, and at other times I regarded him in my heart as my Father, as my God.

Brother Lawrence of the Resurrection

Let us imagine that within us is an extremely rich palace, built entirely of gold and precious stones.... Imagine, too, as is indeed so, that you have a part to play in order for the palace to be so beautiful.... Imagine, also, that in this palace dwells this mighty King who has been gracious enough to become your Father; and that he is seated upon an extremely valuable throne, which is your heart....

All of this imagining is necessary that we may truly understand that within us lies something incomparably more precious than what we see outside ourselves....

In my opinion, if I had understood as I do now that in this little palace of my soul dwells so great a King, I would not have left him alone so often.

St. Teresa of Avila

Things to Think About

In addition to using our imaginations, we can pray "by using our ability to think and reflect," said St. Jane Frances de Chantal. We can consider the virtues our Lord demonstrated during his life on earth—among others, his humility, patience, kindness, love of enemies. As we think about these things, our wills will be moved and touched by God, giving rise to strong stirrings of the heart. These should lead to some practical resolutions for daily life.

I want you to go fishing sometimes. How? I will tell you. The most holy passion of Jesus is a sea of sorrows but, at the same time, a sea of love. Pray to God that he teach you to fish in this sea. Then dive into its depths. No matter how deep you go, you will never reach bottom.

St. Paul of the Cross

Try meditating on each word of the Our Father, in the manner St. Ignatius of Loyola describes: Our position ... can be kneeling or sitting, whichever seems to be more conducive to praying and better fitted to our own devotion. We take care to keep our attention focused in this method of praying by taking advantage of a help like keeping our eyes closed or fixing our gaze upon some one place or object. As we begin our consideration, we say "Father," and we let this word remain within us for so long a time as we find meanings, comparisons, relish, and consolation coming from our reflection upon this word. We act in a similar way with every word of the Our Father or of any prayer we may want to pray in this method....

When one word or two of the prayer, Our Father, occupies our full attention with relish and consolation, we do not hurry on.... We may spend a whole hour of prayer on one word or two of the Our Father.

Beyond Thinking

Spiritual reading can provide good subject matter for meditation, said St. Claude la Colombière, but don't get too attached to what you're reading.

If you find good in it, don't change. [But] remember that every time you are filled with exceptional feelings, either of thanksgiving, or the love of God, or of admiration for his kindnesses, or of desire to please him, or of contempt for the things of earth, or finally, of his presence, you should make them the subject of your prayers....

Enjoy, prolong, increase the desire that God gives you of doing something for him. Make that the subject of your prayer as often as you feel moved by these thoughts.

Always prepare your mind for prayer by choosing a subject for meditation.... When your heart is moved and feels drawn to speak to God, to love him and converse with him, consider quietly and with loving respect his divine Majesty's wishes in your regard; and then, instead of meditating, think only of obeying him.

Blessed Marie of the Incarnation

Meditation is the mother of the love of God, and contemplation is the daughter of the love of God....
Contemplation is nothing other than taking delight in the
goodness of him whom we have learned to know in meditation, and whom we have learned to love by means of
this knowledge.

St. Francis de Sales

SEVEN

STRUGGLES AND SNAGS

Next time you feel discouraged because your prayer is dry, difficult, and devoid of God's presence, think of St. Jane Frances de Chantal. She said her own prayer life was "ordinarily nothing but distraction and a little suffering."

"Little"? When pressed to describe that suffering, Jane used phrases like "spiritual nausea," "a confused turmoil of darkness and helplessness," "feelings of rebellion, doubts, and every other sort of horror." This was no passing phase either. Writing toward the end of her life, this outwardly serene and cheerful woman confided that she had endured her trials "for forty-one years now."

Providentially, St. Jane had the best of spiritual directors to help her navigate this spiritual minefield—none other than St. Francis de Sales. She met him in 1604, two and a half years after her husband's death in a hunting accident. Overwhelmed with grief, Jane had refocused and had adopted a rule of life that gave all her time to prayer, works of mercy, and the care and teaching of her four children. When St. Francis became her confessor, it was the beginning of an extraordinarily fruitful friendship that led, in time, to their cofounding the Visitation Order.

Francis told Jane how to handle her temptations to doubt. Treat them like bees, he advised. "Don't fear them, don't touch them, and they won't hurt you. Pass on and don't spend time with them. You can be absolutely convinced that all the temptations of hell can't possibly stain a soul that doesn't love them."

Jane learned fast and passed along similar advice in her own letters of spiritual direction. "Do you know that these fears and self-torturings are pure temptations of the devil?" she wrote to a struggling nun. "Make a firm stand and take no heed of them, dear daughter, for the devil is only trying in his malice to deceive you. Pay no attention to anything the tempter suggests. Throw yourself on the mercy of the divine Mercy."

Never completely delivered from her temptations and sense of spiritual dryness, St. Jane learned to bear with them out of love for God. We can judge the results from this assessment by St. Vincent de Paul, who knew Jane well: "I consider her one of the holiest souls I've ever met."

Distracted?

Leave at the door of the place where you are going to converse with God all extraneous thoughts, saying, with St. Bernard, "O my thoughts, wait here. After prayer we shall speak about other matters."

St. Alphonsus Liguori

Thomas of Celano recounts an instance when St. Francis of Assisi took vigorous action against a particular source of distraction.

One Lent he had made a little vase.... One day, while he was devoutly saying the Divine Office, his eyes turned to look at the vessel, and he felt that the interior man was thereby impeded in its fervor. Sorrowful therefore that the voice of his heart had been interrupted in its speaking to the ears of God, ... he said before the listening brothers, "Alas, what a worthless work that has such power over me that it can twist my mind to itself! I will sacrifice it to the Lord, whose sacrifice it has impeded." When he said these words, he took the little vase and threw it into the fire to be burned. "Let us be ashamed," he said, "to be caught up by worthless imaginings, for at the time of prayer we speak to the *great King.*"

The very pains we take to prevent distractions often work upon us as a considerable distraction.... If you begin to reflect and to turn your eyes upon self in order to learn what sort of attitude you are maintaining as you gaze upon God, then it is no longer upon him that your gaze is fixed but upon your own conduct and upon yourself.

St. Jane Frances de Chantal

Who among us would put up with the behavior of a friend who addressed him but then turned away to speak to another person when we were about to reply?... Yet God puts up with the hearts of so many of us who pray while thinking about different things.... So then, should we despair of the human race and say that everyone whose prayer has been interrupted by wandering thoughts is condemned? If we say this, my brethren, I do not know what hope remains for any of us. But since we do hope in God because his mercy is great, let us say to him, "To you, O Lord, I lift up my soul" (Ps 86:4).

And how have I lifted it up?

As best I could, Lord, according to the strength you gave me to catch it when it fled away.

And I can imagine the Lord saying, "Yes, but ... every time you stood before me, you had such-and-such vain and empty thoughts and have hardly offered me a single word of undistracted prayer."

Yet I would answer, "'But you, Lord, are good and forgiving' (Ps 86:5).... It is only because I am sick that my thoughts wander away. Heal me, and I shall stand firm. Strengthen me, and my attention will be fixed. But until you do, put up with me. 'For you, O Lord, are good and forgiving.'"

St. Augustine

Distractions can be a means of purification.

As regards prayer, it is not less profitable to us or less pleasing to God when it is full of distractions. On the contrary, it will perhaps be more useful to us than if we had much consolation in it, because there will be more labor—provided, however, that we are faithful in withdrawing from these distractions, and in refraining from dwelling on them voluntarily.

St. Francis de Sales

The whole aim of one who is beginning to pray, and do not forget this, for it is very important, must be to work and resolve and dispose herself with the utmost diligence to conform her will with the will of God.... Very often the Lord wills that evil thoughts and aridities should persecute and afflict us, without our being able to rid ourselves of them, and sometimes he even allows the reptiles to bite us, so that we may know how to protect ourselves better in the future, and to prove whether we are truly sorry for having offended him.

Therefore, if you fall sometimes, you must not be discouraged, nor slacken your efforts to make progress, for God can extract good even from these falls.... Place all your confidence in the mercy of God, and not in yourselves, and you will see how his Majesty will ... bring you into a land where these wild beasts will neither touch nor annoy you.

St. Teresa of Avila

Oh, the great illusion ... to imagine that one has little or much virtue, according as one has few or many distractions in prayer. I have known nuns who were raised to a high degree of contemplation, and who were distracted from the beginning right to the end of their prayer.... Even though you were ravished in ecstasy twenty-four times a day, even though I had twenty-four distractions in reciting a Hail Mary, if I were as humble and as mortified as you, I would not wish to exchange my involuntary distractions for your ecstasies devoid of merit. In a word, I do not recognize perfection where there is no mortification.

St. Claude la Colombière

Parched and Prayerless

There are people who want experiences of God's closeness in prayer as a means of gaining perfection.... Nevertheless he permits them to be dry and parched, powerless and blind to the extent that they don't even know what they're doing. Well then, let's look for our perfection in this darkness and obscurity, by humility, patience, and resignation.... Seek peace in the midst of your trial, calm your mind in the midst of your restlessness by seeing the will of God in these things and by bending to his good pleasure. This will prepare you to receive the peace you desire so strongly.... Practice faithfully the holy teaching of our father, St. Francis de Sales, to *refuse nothing* that God's providence presents for our perfection and to *desire nothing* that is not given us.

St. Jane Frances de Chantal

St. Francis de Sales understood that many of us go through periods when prayer and meditation feel joyless and boring. "Don't be the slightest bit upset!" is his first bit of advice. Here is more:

Open the door to vocal prayer from time to time. Tell the Lord how unhappy you are about your sorry state. Acknowledge your unworthiness. Beg him to help you. Kiss his picture, if you have one, and speak to him these words of Jacob: "I will not let you go, unless you bless me" (Gn 32:26).... At other times, take a book and read it attentively until your spirit is awakened and renewed. Stir up your heart sometimes by some gesture or attitude of external devotion: prostrate yourself on the ground, cross your hands over your breast, venerate a crucifix....

If you receive no comfort after all this, don't worry, no matter how great your dryness. Just remain before your God in a devout attitude. How many courtiers enter the prince's chambers a hundred times a year with no hope of speaking to him, but just to be seen by him and to do their duty! This is how we should come to prayer ... purely and simply to do our duty and show our fidelity.

Sometimes when I find myself spiritually in dryness so great that I cannot produce a single good thought, I recite very slowly an Our Father or a Hail Mary. These prayers alone console me. They nourish my soul.

St. Thérèse of Lisieux

Dryness and aridity ... may be a trial sent from God. Bear it patiently. Remain humbly at his feet. Assure him simply that you wish only what is pleasing to him.

When it happens that you find yourself in this state of trouble, you must seriously examine whether it does not point to some secret fault which you do not really want to give up.... Ask yourself if your pride is really conquered, your self-love really under control. Do you not still want to be highly thought of? Do you submit your judgment to the yoke of obedience? Do you fulfill your duties faithfully and exactly? Do you try to perform your spiritual exercises with attention and in a spirit of faith? Do you still easily give in to venial faults?... Then appeal to the Divine Physician of souls asking him to help you to see your spiritual weaknesses and to grant you the grace to remedy them. Confide entirely in the power and goodness of God, and thus you will be able to offer yourself entirely to him in the fervor and recollection of meditation.

St. Mary Euphrasia Pelletier

If the tediousness that assails is very great, divide your meditation into several parts, and employ yourself mainly in petitions to God.... It's enough to repeat, "My Jesus, mercy. Lord, have mercy on us."

St. Alphonsus Liguori

Dark Nights

In meditation, prayer, Communion, I find no soul. In that tabernacle I know he is, but I see it not, feel not. A thousand deaths might hang over me to compel me to deny his presence there, and I would embrace them all rather than deny it an instant. Yet it seems that he is not there for me.

St. Elizabeth Ann Seton

When people have been growing in virtue and persevering in prayer for a time, says St. John of the Cross, God leads them into deeper prayer by allowing them to undergo a "dark night of the soul" in which he seems very far away. They struggle to pray as they used to, "but this trouble that they are taking is quite useless," says St. John: "God is now leading them by another road, which is that of contemplation, and it is very different from the first."

It is well for those who find themselves in this condition to take comfort, to persevere in patience and to be in no wise afflicted. Let them trust in God, who abandons not those that seek him with a simple and right heart, and will not fail to give them what is needful for the road, until he bring them into the clear and pure light of love....

The way in which they are to conduct themselves in this night of sense is to devote themselves not at all to reasoning and meditation, since this is not the time for it, but to allow the soul to remain in peace and quietness, although it may seem clear to them that they are doing nothing and are wasting their time, and although it may appear to them that it is because of their weakness that they have no desire in that state to think of anything. The truth is that they will be doing quite sufficient if they have patience and persevere in prayer without making any effort.

I thank my Jesus for making me walk in darkness. In it I am wrapped in profound peace.

St. Thérèse of Lisieux

Therefore during this time of suffering and desolation I say to God: "My Lord, let the world and even the devil take for themselves what I cannot prevent them having, but they shall never have anything to do with my heart, my will that you have left in my possession—this belongs to you; take it, it is yours, and do what you will with it."

St. Claude la Colombière

This prayer comes from Blessed Henry Suso, whose lengthy stretches of spiritual darkness rival the dryness St. Jane de Chantal experienced.

My soul has longed for you all night, O Eternal Wisdom! And in the early morning I turn to you from the depths of my heart. May your holy presence remove all dangers from my soul and body. May your many graces fill the inmost recesses of my heart, and inflame it with your divine love.

On Guard!

St. Peter warns us that "the devil prowls around like a roaring lion, seeking someone to devour" (1 Pt 5:8). It seems our adversary sees prayer time as one of his favorite occasions for attack.

Often during the time scheduled for prayer the devil comes with all sorts of struggles and annoyances.... He does this to make you weary of holy prayer.... But prayer is a weapon with which you can defend yourself against every enemy. If you hold it with love's hand and the arm of free choice, this weapon ... will be your defense.

St. Catherine of Siena

When the enemy wants to challenge me, I conduct myself valiantly. Knowing that to fight a duel is an unworthy act, I turn my back on the adversary without ever looking him in the face. Then I run to my Jesus.

St. Thérèse of Lisieux

If sleeping during prayer becomes a habit, then we should, in order to get rid of it, stand upright, kiss the floor, or renew our attention from time to time. If we do not remedy this bad habit, it will return daily. Are you aware that there is a devil whose business it is to put people to sleep when they are at prayer?

St. Vincent de Paul

The devil is never more busy to distract us with the thoughts of worldly cares than when he perceives us praying and asking God for grace.... And why? Because the enemy sees that at no other time do we gain so many treasures of heavenly goods as when we pray....

We should always be crying to God to aid us.... What does it cost to say, My God, help me! Lord, assist me! Have mercy on me! Is there anything more easy than this? And this little will suffice to save us, if we are diligent in doing it.

St. Alphonsus Liguori

Never abandon prayer because you think you are no good at it. Do not be astonished, those of you who are newcomers, to see a month, two months, three months, six months pass by without any advance. No, not even a year or two years or three! And do not cease to go to prayer as if you were making a great advance in it. St. Teresa [of Avila] was twenty years without being able to pray.... And at the end of twenty years, God rewarded her perseverance.... How do you know ... but that God wishes to make St. Teresas of you? How do you know what reward he may wish to bestow on your perseverance?...

Ask God to give you the grace of prayer,... ask him ceaselessly. It is an alms that you beg of him. It is not possible, if you persevere, for him to refuse you.

St. Vincent de Paul

EIGHT

TRY THIS

When you love someone, you're always on the lookout for ways to express your affection: thoughtful gifts, tender words, acts of kindness, attentive listening. The saints are people who related to God like this in their prayer life. Watching them at prayer, we see loving creativity at work.

A late thirteenth-century document gives us a privileged look at some of St. Dominic's ways of praying. Written by an anonymous author, it was based on eyewitness information from men and women in the religious communities Dominic founded. Since body language was an important aspect of his prayer, early manuscripts of "The Nine Ways of Prayer of St. Dominic" included miniature drawings illustrating his various prayer postures. Here are six of the "nine ways."

First Way: Dominic, "standing erect, bowed his head and humbly considering Christ, his Head, compared his lowliness with the excellence of Christ." Aloud, he offered prayers like, "Lord, I am not worthy to have you come under my roof" (Mt 8:8).

Second Way: "Throwing himself outstretched upon the ground, lying on his face," St. Dominic wept for his own and others' sins, using words like "'God, be merciful to me, a sinner'" (Lk 18:13).

Fourth Way: Dominic liked to stand before a crucifix and look at it "with perfect attention" and frequent genuflections.

Fifth Way: "Often his hands would be extended before his breast in the manner of an open book," as if he were reading in God's presence. "He would sometimes join his hands, clasping them firmly together. At other times he would raise his hands to his shoulders as the priest does at Mass."

Sixth Way: St. Dominic sometimes prayed standing, "with his hands and arms outstretched forcefully in the form of a cross."

Seventh Way: Often he reached up, "like an arrow which has been shot from a taut bow straight upwards into the sky." Sometimes his upraised hands were joined, other times, "slightly separated as if about to receive something from heaven."

By example and instruction, St. Dominic "constantly taught the friars to pray in this way," urging them on with psalm verses like "Come, bless the Lord, all you servants of the Lord!... Lift up your hands, ... and bless the Lord" (Ps 134:1, 2).

The Wings of Prayer

If you want your prayers to fly to God, equip them with the two wings of fasting and almsgiving.

St. Augustine

Fasting gives us devotion and confidence at prayer. And notice how prayer and fasting assist each other like two allies, according to what is written: "When a brother helps a brother, both shall be comforted" (Prv 18:19). Prayer obtains the strength for fasting, and fasting merits the grace to pray. Fasting renders prayer more powerful, and prayer responds by sanctifying the fast and presenting it to the Lord.

St. Bernard of Clairvaux

St. Angela Merici instructed her followers to fast.

For Scripture says, "Prayer is good with fasting" (see Tb 12:8). And in the Bible we read, "Anna, daughter of Phanuel, who day and night served God in the temple with fasting and prayer" (Lk 2:37). And as by fasting we mortify the carnal appetites and the senses, so by prayer we beg God for the true grace of spiritual life.

He who wishes to pray without mortifying himself is like a bird trying to fly before it has feathers.

St. Philip Neri

Prayer knocks at the door, fasting obtains, mercy receives. Prayer, mercy, and fasting: these three are one and they give life to each other.

Fasting is the soul of prayer, mercy is the lifeblood of fasting. Let no one try to separate them, they cannot be separated. If you have only one of them or not all together, you have nothing. So if you pray, fast; if you fast, show mercy; if you want your petition to be heard, hear the petition of others. If you do not close your ear to others, you open God's ear to yourself.

St. Peter Chrysologus

Picture This

Looking for a prayer partner? Picture Jesus beside you, says St. Teresa of Avila.

Imagine that this Lord himself is at your side and see how lovingly and how humbly he is teaching you—and believe me, you should stay with so good a Friend for as long as you can before you leave him. If you become accustomed to having him at your side, and if he sees that you love him to be there and are always trying to please him, you will never be able, as we put it, to send him away, nor will he ever fail you. He will help you in all your trials and you will have him everywhere. Do you think it is a small thing to have such a Friend as that beside you?

Imagine Christ our Lord before you, hanging upon the cross. Speak with him of how, being the Creator, he then became man and how, possessing eternal life, he submitted to temporal death to die for our sins.

Then I shall meditate upon myself and ask, "What have I done for Christ? What am I now doing for Christ?" As I see him in this condition, hanging upon the cross, I shall meditate on the thoughts that come to my mind.

St. Ignatius Loyola

Growing up, St. Anthony Mary Claret loved to pray in church before an image of Our Lady of the Rosary.

I talked and prayed so trustingly that I was quite sure the Blessed Virgin heard me. I used to imagine a sort of wire running from the image in front of me to its heavenly original. Although I had not yet seen a telegraph line at that time, I had imagined how it would be to have a telegraph line to heaven.

Some of the young women who joined the Sisters of Charity were illiterate and thought this might be an obstacle to meditation. Not at all, St. Vincent de Paul told them. Until they learned to read the Gospels, they could use visual aids.

Have in your hands pictures of the mysteries you intend to meditate on. While looking at them, you may think, "What is that? What's the meaning of that?" And so your mind will be opened.

A servant of God used to pray in this way. Looking at a picture of the Blessed Virgin, she considered the eyes, and said: "What use did you make of your eyes, O Blessed Mother?" And an interior voice replied: ... "I took great pleasure in beholding my Son; and while looking at him I was raised to the love of God...."

Anyone can pray like this, said St. Vincent. "All you need is an image or a picture. Our Lord will surely say something to you."

St. Teresa of Avila liked to meditate on images of Christ and scenes from his earthly life. She recommended the practice to others: "Try to carry about an image or painting of this Lord that is to your liking, not so as to carry it about on your heart and never look at it but so as to speak often with him; for he will inspire you with what to say." She herself returned again and again to Jesus' conversation with the woman at the well (see Jn 4:4-42):

Oh, how many times do I recall the living water that the Lord told the Samaritan woman about! And so I am very fond of that gospel passage. Thus it is, indeed, that from the time I was a little child, without understanding this good as I do now, I often begged the Lord to give me the water. I always carried with me a painting of this episode of the Lord at the well, with the words, inscribed: *Domine, da mihi aquam....* "Lord, give me water."

Creative Expressions

St. Philip Neri had some prayers set to music. Many other saints—including those who belonged to religious communities that chant the psalms—sang their prayers. Fr. Solanus Casey, a Franciscan, was one of these. But he also had a more unusual way of making a joyful noise. Each Sunday evening for about a half-hour, Solanus took his fiddle to the chapel and played hymns before the Blessed Sacrament.

Speaking of himself as "he," St. Ignatius of Loyola describes the journal he started writing immediately after his conversion—an aid for meditating on ideas that had struck him in his spiritual reading.

He greatly enjoyed his books, and the idea struck him to copy down, in abridged form, the more important items in the life of Christ and of the saints.... He set about writing these things in a book, taking great care and using red ink for Christ's words and blue for those of Our Lady. He used polished and lined paper and wrote in a good hand since he had an attractive penmanship. He spent some of his time in writing and some in prayer.... The result of all this was that he felt within himself a strong impulse to serve our Lord.

I shall meditate as I have been accustomed, in the little Italian church on Twelfth Street, by the side of the open window, looking out at the plants growing on the roof, the sweet corn, the boxes of herbs, the geraniums in bright bloom, and I shall rest happy in the presence of Christ on the altar, and then I shall come home and I shall write ... and try to catch some of these things that happen to bring me nearer to God, to catch them and put them down on paper.

Dorothy Day

You don't know what to say to Our Lord in prayer. Nothing comes to you and yet you would like to ask his advice about many things.

Look: take some notes during the day of the things you want to think about in the presence of God. And then go with those notes to pray.

Blessed Josemaría Escrivá de Balaguer

Besides keeping prayer journals, many saints jotted down prayers or meditations. In this one, Blessed Frederic Ozanam expresses his thanks for the graces that usually go unnoticed.

We are not sufficiently grateful for God's little blessings. We thank him for having created and redeemed us and given us good parents and a wife and beloved children, and for giving himself to us so often in the sacrament of the altar. But besides these powerful graces,... how many more subtle ones are woven into the fabric of our lives!

There was the steady friend I met during my first year at college, who inspired rather than corrupted me; there was the older man who gave me a fatherly welcome and the woman who gave me good advice.... And even smaller things—an inspiration that prompted me to visit some poor people on a day when I was in a bad mood; seeing the appalling indignity of their situation, I went home ashamed at my imaginary woes. How often it happens that some inconvenience—say, a boring visitor I'd gladly wish away to Hong Kong—gives me an opportunity to do someone some good!

St. Philip Neri loved to say short prayers over and over, lingering over each word with great fervor. To better concentrate on the meaning of the Hail Mary, he condensed it into a single sentence—"Virgin Mary, Mother of God, pray to Jesus for me"—and made up a rosary consisting of sixty-three repetitions of this prayer. Another chaplet featured short prayers composed by Philip—simple, ardent statements to be said aloud, with feeling. Here are a few of those prayers, as handed down by one of his friends.

—My Jesus, don't trust me.

—My God, I wish to learn the road to heaven.

—What can I do, my Jesus, to please you?

—Holy Trinity, one God, have mercy on me.

—I seek you and do not find you. Come to me, my Jesus.

—I want to love you, my Jesus, but I don't know how.

—My Jesus, if you don't help me, I'm ruined.

—I distrust myself, but I trust in you, my Jesus.

Variety, the Spice of Prayer

There is nothing laid down about our posture in prayer, provided the soul keeps its attention when present with God. We ourselves stand when we pray, after the example of the publican, "who stood a long way off" (Lk 18:13). We also bend the knee, in accordance with what we read in the Acts of the Apostles (see Acts 7:59; 20:36); and we pray sitting, as you see in the case of David (1 Chr 17:16).... And unless it were right to pray lying down the psalmist would not have said, "I will water my bed with my tears" (Ps 7:7).

St. Augustine

St. Gregory of Sinai recommended variety in the manner of saying the Jesus Prayer: "Jesus Christ, Son of God, have mercy on me, a sinner."

Some teach the saying of the prayer with the lips, others with and in the mind. In my opinion both are advisable. For at times the mind, left to itself, becomes wearied and too exhausted to say the prayer mentally; at other times the lips get tired of this work. Therefore both methods of prayer should be used—with the lips and with the mind.

... But Keep Your Focus

Haphazard reading, constantly varied and as if lighted upon by chance, does not edify but makes the mind unstable; taken into the memory lightly, it goes out from it even more lightly. But you should concentrate on certain authors and let your mind grow accustomed to them.

William of St. Thierry

We owe much to those who in what they wrote enlightened our understanding.... But the book which speaks to the understanding but also awakens the will to the love of God should be held in high esteem. Hardly ever should we allow it to leave our hands. It should be read with the mind in repose, doing violence to oneself to pay attention, and casting aside every other thought.

Do not go jumping about from one book to another, nor begin by reading the end. For as a philosopher said, we enjoy variety in what we read, but perseverance in reading is what brings us profit. You should always pick out certain passages from what you have read and fix them in your mind.... Always have a definite time each day for reading, just as you should have for prayer and contemplation.

Blessed Alphonsus de Orozco

It's good to come away from prayer with a practical resolution for the day, agrees Blessed John Gabriel Perboyre. Just don't bite off more than you can chew.

Be certain that if you make two resolutions you make one too many; and that if you make a new one every day, the end of the year will find you with all your faults and with nothing to offer our Lord but a mountain of infidelities. If St. Francis de Sales and St. Vincent de Paul had made new resolutions each morning, St. Francis would never have acquired the gentleness that won every heart, nor would St. Vincent have become a model of humility. It is important, you see, always to make the same resolution until we have perfectly overcome the fault we are combating or have acquired the virtue we desire.... Every day we should renew our resolution in our morning prayers, that it may be kept fresh and vigorous.

People who try every dish at a banquet, eating a little of each, disorder their stomachs so much that they can't sleep.... So it is with people who wish to try every method and means that might lead them to perfection.... A certain discomfort and indigestion follows. This deprives them of peace and serenity of mind in our Lord's presence—the "one thing needed" which Mary chose, and "which will not be taken away from her" (Lk 10:42).

St. Francis de Sales

NINE

PRAYER'S BEST TEACHER

I am the mortal enemy of what is called 'direction,'" one of the twentieth century's most skilled spiritual directors wrote a friend in 1906. "The Holy Ghost alone can form souls."

Blessed Columba Marmion, an Irish-born monk and future abbot of the Benedictine Abbey of Maredsous in Belgium, wasn't trying to shock or to depreciate the help that comes from wise spiritual counselors. He was merely making the point that growth in prayer is mainly God's work.

Other saints said the same. "Don't suppose that prayer is a work of the human mind," said Francis de Sales. "It's a special gift of the Holy Spirit." And to a woman who wanted a method for mental prayer, Philip Neri said, "Be humble and obedient and the Holy Spirit will teach you."

Abbot Marmion himself was a student in this school of prayer. "I have a great desire to be guided, led, moved by the Spirit of Jesus in all things," he wrote. One reason for his eagerness is that he had already experienced the Spirit's transforming power. As a student walking into a study hall one ordinary day, the young Marmion had received a sudden "light on the infinity of God." It was a pivotal instant that shaped his relationship with God for the rest of his life.

In books like his classic *Christ the Life of the Soul*, Abbot

Marmion stressed the need not just to imitate Christ but to be transformed in Christ. This is a job for the Holy Spirit, he stressed, and obviously beyond human doing: "St. Paul tells us quite plainly that we cannot even pronounce the name of Jesus without the Holy Spirit (1 Cor 12:3). With much greater reason, we are incapable, without the help of this Divine Artist, of reproducing in our souls the features of the heavenly Model."

Columba Marmion's advice to us: See your prayer life as the Spirit's work from start to finish. Learn to recognize his voice. Follow his inspirations. Pray constantly to receive him.

You may perhaps say: Have we not already received the Holy Spirit at Baptism, and yet more specially in the sacrament of Confirmation? Assuredly we have, but we can always receive him more abundantly. We can always receive from him clearer light, greater strength. He can always make deeper wellsprings of consolation rise up in our souls, and enkindle within our hearts a more intense love.

The Spirit of Love Teaches Us

The Holy Spirit is the master of prayer. It is not surprising that God has given us this master to teach us the difficult lessons of prayer, since prayer is a supernatural work of love. There is no prayer which is not a work of love....

Père Jacques (Lucien-Louis Bunel)

During Pentecost Mass in 1623, St. Louise de Marillac experienced an outpouring of grace that ended a period of spiritual anguish and made her vividly aware of the Spirit's power and action. From then on, says biographer J. Calvet, she was a "disciple of the Holy Spirit" and turned to him "as towards that love which would make her worthy of the Father by making her more like the Son." Said Louise: The Holy Spirit "fills us with pure love of God.... The Spirit makes us obedient to God, so that we may share the divine life."

St. Louise marked this anniversary for the rest of her life with a yearly Ascension-to-Pentecost retreat. Some of us may want to follow her example by using the same ten days in prayerful preparation for welcoming the Spirit of love more completely.

It is this Holy Spirit which will light in our hearts the flame of love.... How many know this Spirit of Love? And yet he alone is the source of their whole interior life.

Blessed Columba Marmion

The Holy Spirit is the teacher of prayer. He enables us to live in perfect peace and constant joy, which is a foretaste of paradise.

St. Philip Neri

I think that for certain people, our blessed Master takes on the task of doing everything by himself. Real spiritual direction is a precious thing, but it is very rare. One can be comforted, upheld, and guided by a holy priest, but without finding the fullness of the guidance that our Lord sometimes reserves for himself. There are depths of soul which he alone can penetrate. He alone knows us fully, with all our unknown weaknesses, hopes, and misunderstood needs.

What we should ask from our spiritual director—in all humility, simplicity, and obedience—is a bit more light on our troubles, advice for our overall approach to our spiritual life, comfort in times of discouragement or suffering. But only in the heart of Jesus do we find the definitive support, deep strength, and total understanding of our soul and its needs that enable us to progress and advance towards him.

Elisabeth Leseur

The great method for mental prayer is simply this: that there is none when the Holy Spirit has taken charge of the person who is meditating, for then he does with the soul as it pleases him, and all rules and methods vanish away. In the hands of God the soul must become like clay in the hands of a potter ...; or, if you like, the soul must become like soft wax receptive to the impression of a seal, or like a blank sheet upon which the Holy Spirit writes his divine will. If, when entering upon prayer, we could make ourselves a mere capacity for receiving the Spirit of God, this would suffice for all method. Prayer must be carried on by grace, and not by deliberate art.

St. Jane Frances de Chantal

From a letter to St. Francis Borgia:

For each one, that meditation is the best in which God communicates himself the most. For God knows and sees what is most suitable for us, and knowing all, he himself points out the way to be followed. But first we have to grope dimly, before finding this way, which will lead us to the life that has no end where we shall enjoy the most holy gifts of God.

St. Ignatius of Loyola

God wants us to pray whenever we're in difficulty, said Venerable Charles de Foucauld, and in those moments the Spirit leads us to pray in one of two ways:

We can, like our Lord at Gethsemane, let nature speak and ask God to deliver us from suffering, danger, or need, but in that case we must add immediately, as our Lord did, "Nevertheless, let it be as you, not I, would have it" (Mt 26:39). Or we could, silencing nature and letting only our faith and love of God speak, simply cry out, "Our Father in heaven, may your name be held holy" (Mt 6:9), make anything happen as long as it is for your greatest glory. Do what you want with me, I only ask you for one thing, glorify your name to the utmost! Both prayers are good; God gives us the example of both.... The Holy Spirit gives us an inclination toward one or the other; we only need to follow this inclination.

Listen to His Voice

Let us now consider what help to do good we receive from "the good Spirit" (Lk 11:13). He admonishes us, he moves us, he instructs us. He admonishes our memory (Jn 15:26), he moves our will, he instructs our reason.... He suggests what is good to the memory in holy meditations, and thus banishes from our minds cowardice and sloth....

As often as you become conscious of these promptings to good in your hearts, give glory to God and reverence the Holy Spirit whose voice is sounding in your ears.

St. Bernard of Clairvaux

I recommend a great fidelity to the movements of the Holy Spirit. Your baptism and your confirmation have established him as a living fountain in your soul. Hear his whisperings, and put the other inspirations to flight at once. If you are faithful in this, little by little this divine Spirit will become your guide and bear you with him into God's bosom. The Holy Spirit holds the place for us that Jesus did for his apostles during his mortal life. Just as they could have recourse to him, ... so he has sent us "another Paraclete to stay with us, and teach us all things which he has told us."

Blessed Columba Marmion

St. Frances Cabrini prayed constantly to the Holy Spirit and said that the descent of the Holy Spirit was the mystery of the rosary she loved most. This exhortation, written during an 1894 Genoa-to-New York sea journey, is typical:

Let us be faithful to the operations of the Holy Spirit in our souls! Let our minds be pure, disinterested, humble, pliant, and then we shall see what beautiful and wonderful things the Holy Spirit will work in our souls.... This Spirit works within us, inspires us, instructs us, encourages us, and comforts us with his abundant and perennial lights, with his promptings and impulse in every holy work.... From this we are able to understand that if we are not holy it is through our own fault.

If only we would receive God's inspirations to their fullest extent, ... in no time we should be making great strides in holiness, heaven knows! However full a cistern is, it waters the garden only in proportion to the size of the pipes leading from it. The Holy Spirit, source of living water, embraces the heart of man to pour out his graces into it. However, he means us freely to consent to accept them, so he infuses them only as he pleases, and to the extent that we are disposed to cooperate with them....

This is the idea behind St. Paul's appeal: "We entreat you not to offer God's grace an ineffectual welcome" (2 Cor 6:1). If medicine were to be placed in a sick man's hand but he did not put it into his mouth, ... it would do him no good. We too offer God's grace an ineffectual welcome if, when it is poured out in our hearts, we do not consent to it....

St. Francis de Sales

What the Holy Spirit did for the apostles he will do for us.
Blessed André Bessette

Deeper Into Prayer

When we are faithful, every day, to consecrate a time, longer or shorter according to our aptitudes and duties of state, in speaking with the heavenly Father, in gathering up his inspirations and listening to what the Holy Spirit brings to mind, then the words of Christ ... go on multiplying, inundating the soul with divine light and opening out in it fountains of life....

Prayer then becomes a state, and the soul can find its God at will, even in the midst of many occupations.... This state is more than the simple presence of God. It is an intimate intercourse, full of love, in which the soul speaks to God, sometimes with the lips, most often from the heart, and remains intimately united to him, despite the variety of the day's work and occupations. There are many souls, simple and upright, who, faithful to the attractions of the Holy Spirit, reach this desirable state.

Blessed Columba Marmion

Led by the Spirit, some people experience a kind of prayer that no human effort can produce.

God grants it to whom he pleases, when he pleases, and in the way he pleases. Man cannot teach it, nor can he attain to it by his own labor and effort. In this prayer the soul without any impulse of its own finds itself filled suddenly with light and holy love, and given understanding of certain truths which are incomprehensible to any other than itself.

St. Vincent de Paul

Following an intense experience of God's love, Blessed Marie of the Incarnation found herself drawn into intimate conversation with God.

I was only twenty at this time, and my son was not yet a year old. My father asked me to come back and live at home; there it was easier to find some solitude. I lived on the top floor where, as I did some quiet needlework, my mind was occupied in its usual activity and my heart spoke constantly to God. I myself was astonished at the things my heart said; it spoke not at my prompting but was moved by a higher power.... It was absolutely incomprehensible to me that my heart should speak to him so intimately and so eloquently. But far from setting myself against it, I allowed myself to follow this attraction....

It must be acknowledged that the Spirit of God is a great teacher! Although I had never been instructed about mental prayer and mortification—I didn't even know these terms—he taught me everything, allowing me to experience the one and practice the other.... My heart poured out words of thanks, of praise of God,.... of loving repentance, of pledges of fidelity in following whatever the Divine Goodness wanted of me.

St. Charles of Sezze describes the moment when the Spirit brought him into "another kind of prayer, more interior and heartfelt":
Our Lord started showing me his mercy in this manner when one day I was praying before a painting of the Madonna in the church of the Jesuit Fathers in Sezze.... The image became so fixed in my heart and mind that I was completely inflamed with love.... I was changed into another person, losing thought and intellect in the divine light. Like one dazed I rested in my enjoyment and my soul was very content.

The change that came over me through this kind of prayer was very great. By the divine grace in it I was interiorly taught to do everything for God, and I came to understand that without divine help our works are really nothing and have no value, even though performed with all possible exactness.

Come, Holy Spirit!

I have prayed for you, that you too may be granted that great Spirit of fire, whom I have received. If you wish to receive him, so that he dwells in you, first offer physical labors and humility of heart and, lifting your thoughts to heaven day and night, seek this Spirit of fire with a righteous heart—and he will be given unto you.

St. Anthony the Great

If you desire to correct your faults, and you feel that you cannot, if you languish with tepidity and it seems you can do no good, but still you wish to be fervent, try to be devout to the Holy Spirit, invoking him often and with your whole hearts. Stir up in yourselves strong desires to receive him, repeat often to him: "Create in me a clean heart, Lord, and put a new and right spirit within me. Do not cast me away from your presence, and do not take your holy Spirit from me" (Ps 51:10-11). If you invoke him with a humble and trusting heart, filled with good desires, he will descend with his blessed light and inflaming fire. He will come and penetrate into the very center of your heart, purifying it, changing it, enlightening it, inflaming it, and consuming it with the flames of his holy and divine love.

St. Frances Cabrini

O you who are adorable, tremendous, blessed, give him to us! Send forth your Spirit, and we shall be made, and you will renew the face of the earth! (Ps 103:30).

William of St. Thierry

TEN

PRAY YOUR WAY THROUGH THE DAY

Christians have always sought to "pray without ceasing" (1 Thes 5:17)—that is, to find ways of keeping centered on God between times specifically given to prayer. If you've thought of this as an ideal that's incompatible with the demands of a busy life, you'll be interested in the saintly tips offered below.

Among Eastern Christians, the desire to "pray always" gave rise to the Jesus Prayer: "Lord Jesus Christ, Son of God, have mercy on me, a sinner." Modeled on the petitions of Gospel figures like blind beggars and a desperate mother (see Mt 9:27; 15:22), the Jesus Prayer is a trusting cry for help, constantly repeated at prayer and throughout the day. The seventh-century Palestinian hermit St. John Climacus said that this kind of prayer made present "the remembrance of Jesus ... with each breath." His fourteenth-century disciple St. Gregory of Sinai said that, prayed well, the Jesus Prayer leads to the highest forms of contemplation.

In the Western Church, many Christians have pursued continual prayer through "the practice of the presence of God." A little book by that name has become a spiritual classic. It was written by Brother Lawrence of the Resurrection, a seventeenth-century lay Carmelite who served as cook in a Paris monastery.

Though not canonized, he had a saint's humble holiness and profoundly influenced the many people who sought him out.

As Brother Lawrence describes it, practicing the presence of God means offering him our "simple attention and general, loving gaze." It's "a conscious movement of our souls to God," recalling his constant presence and taking "great pleasure" at the fact. As we go about our daily business, "we can make our heart like a little chapel into which we retire from time to time to converse with God gently, humbly, and lovingly," said Brother Lawrence. "What can be more pleasing to God than to stop whatever we're doing a thousand times a day to worship him in our hearts?"

I like to picture Brother Lawrence in his bustling kitchen, where he said he experienced God "as tranquilly as if I were on my knees before the Blessed Sacrament.... I turn my little omelette in the pan for the love of God. When it is finished, if I have nothing to do, I prostrate myself on the ground and adore my God, who gave me the grace to make it, after which I arise, more content than a king."

Prepare to Meet the Day

Most of us wouldn't come away from a walk in a beautiful garden without having picked a few flowers, observed St. Francis de Sales. Likewise, he said, before leaving our morning meditation, we should pick one or two inspiring thoughts and "remind ourselves of them during the day, breathing in their spiritual fragrance."

Along with this "spiritual bouquet," we should make some

resolutions for pursuing virtue during the day. Get specific, St. Francis advised. "For example, I am firmly determined to change, by my gentleness, the attitude of those who insult me. I shall try to meet them that very day in order to greet them in a friendly way. In case I do not come across them, I will at least speak well of them and pray to God for them."

Those words that struck you when you were praying: engrave them in your memory and recite them slowly many times during the day.

Blessed Josemaría Escrivá de Balaguer

The good thoughts which God gives you in prayer are relics. Gather them carefully together in order to translate them into acts and you will gladden the heart of God.

St. Vincent de Paul

One more counsel from St. Francis de Sales: make a peaceful transition from prayer to the day's activities.

Keep silence for some time if you can, and move your heart very gently from prayer to your occupations. Keep the feelings and good movements of the will produced in you for as long as possible....

You must get used to being able to pass from prayer to all kinds of activities which your occupation and way of life require of you.... The lawyer must be able to pass from prayer to his work in court, the shopkeeper to his business, the married woman to her duties in her family and the bother of her household tasks, with so much gentleness and peacefulness that their minds are not disturbed in any way. Prayer as well as other duties are according to the will of God. So passing from one to the other must be done in a spirit of humility and devotion.

A Chapel in Your Heart

Blessed Raymond of Capua shares the secret of St. Catherine of Siena's unceasing attentiveness to God.

By an impulse of the Holy Spirit, [she] made for herself a secret cell within her own heart, and made up her mind never to go forth from it no matter what the business on which she was engaged.... [She] remained uninterruptedly within the walls of that inner cell of the heart which no one could take from her....

As I write this, old memories stir, and I bring back to mind how again and again she would recommend me when I was engrossed in all the work I had to do and crushed under the weight of it, or when I was about to set out on a journey: "Build yourself a cell within your heart, and never put a foot outside it." At the time I did not see the full implications of these words, but now I study them with a mind more ready to understand.

We can meditate everywhere—at home or elsewhere, even while walking or working.... The person who seeks God will find him always and everywhere. The essential condition ... is solitude of the heart, without which prayer is worthless....

Deserts and caves are not essential to this solitude of the

heart, which consists in being detached from worldly thoughts and desires. Even on the street, at resorts, and in public meetings, people who need to interact with the secular world can possess solitude of heart and continue united with God.

St. Alphonsus Liguori

Writing to her married sister in 1905, Blessed Elizabeth of the Trinity shared a thought from St. John of the Cross: When we're at the deepest center of ourselves, we're in God.

Isn't that simple, isn't it consoling? Through everything, in the midst of your cares as a mother, ... you can withdraw into this solitude to surrender yourself to the Holy Spirit so that he can transform you in God and imprint on your soul the image of the divine Beauty....

Every hour when you think of it ... you can enter into the center of [your] soul where the Divine Guest dwells; you could think of those beautiful words ... "Your body is the temple of the Holy Spirit who dwells within you,"... and of those from the Master: "Remain in me, and I in you."

The Daylong Conversation

God does not ask a great deal of us: a brief remembrance from time to time, a brief act of adoration, occasionally to ask him for his grace or offer him your sufferings, at other times to thank him for the graces he has given you and is giving you. In the midst of your work find consolation in him as often as possible. During your meals and conversations, occasionally lift up your heart to him.... You need not shout out: he is closer to us than we may think.

Everyone is capable of these familiar conversations with God, some more, some less. Let's try. Perhaps he is only looking for the right intention on our part.

Brother Lawrence of the Resurrection

St. Elizabeth Ann Seton gave specific examples of how we might speak to God in various situations.

For instance, when you go to your studies, ... look up to him with sweet complacency, and think: O Lord, how worthless is this knowledge, if it were not for the enlightening of my mind and improving it to thy service; or for being more useful to my fellow-creatures, and enabled to fill the part thy providence may appoint me.

When going into society or mixing with company, appeal to him who sees your heart.... "Oh, keep my heart from all that would separate me from thee."

When you are excited to impatience, think for a moment how much more reason God has to be angry with you than you can have anger against any human being; and yet how constant is his patience and forbearance.

And in every disappointment, great or small, let your dear heart fly direct to him, your dear Savior, throwing yourself in his arms for refuge against every pain and sorrow. He never will leave you or forsake you.

Think about Christ's sufferings as you go about your day, said Blessed Henry Suso. And when you find your thoughts wandering, address him in disarming words like these:

Say: "Alas, my sweet Lord, what are you doing now? Where are you at this moment? Gentle Lord, come to me, sit by me, go with me, and never leave me!"

"What would Jesus do?" Long before people started wearing WWJD bracelets, St. Vincent de Paul was saying that asking Jesus' advice was an additional reason to talk with him all day.

Try to have constant communion with our Lord. Prayer is the source from which you can gain all the directions you need for your task. When any question arises, turn to God, and say to him: "Lord, you who are the source of knowledge, show me what I ought to do in this matter."…

Be very careful to depend completely on the guidance of our Lord. I mean, when you must choose what you will do, ask yourself: "Does this agree with our Lord's teaching?" If you feel it does, hurry to do it; if not, you must decide against it. Whenever there is a possibility of undertaking good work, say to our Lord: "Lord, if you were here, what would you do? How would you teach these people? What kind of comfort would you give to these people who are sick or unhappy?"

Prayer Breaks

Go and find God when you're at the end of your patience and strength, when you feel alone and powerless. Jesus is waiting for you in the chapel. Tell him, "You know well what's going on, my good Jesus. You're the only one I have who knows everything. Come to my help." Then leave, and don't worry about how you'll manage. It's enough that you told God about it. He has a good memory.

Blessed Jeanne Jugan

St. Edith Stein recommended a midday prayer break to seek God's help and perspective: "Then the rest of the day can take its course, under the same effort and strain, perhaps, but in peace." If at all possible, Edith visited Jesus in the Blessed Sacrament—a practice she had encountered before her conversion, at the cathedral in Cologne, Germany.

We went into the cathedral for a few moments, and as we stood there in respectful silence, a woman came in with her shopping basket and knelt down in one of the pews to say a short prayer. That was something completely new to me. In the synagogue, as in the Protestant churches I had visited, people only went in at the time of the service. But here was someone coming into the empty church in the middle of a day's work as if to talk with a friend. I have never been able to forget that.

Let's try not to perform any action without first offering it to God. And whatever we may be doing, let's not allow more than a quarter of an hour to pass without raising our heart to the Lord.... In our spare moments, too—when we're waiting for someone or walking in the garden or lying sick in bed—let's try to unite ourselves to God to the best of our ability.

St. Alphonsus Liguori

How can I remember to raise my heart to God? Easy, said St. Vincent de Paul. Just use the sounds of the clock, and offer a short prayer whenever it strikes—or "beeps," he might say in our age of digital timepieces.

> At night when you retire to rest, take your beads and go off to sleep while saying the rosary. Do the same as little children who fall asleep saying, "Mama, mama."
>
> *St. Bernadette*

Prayer Cues From Daily Life

Everything he saw pointed St. Anthony Mary Claret to God. Flowers brought to mind the virtues God calls us to seek. A tree loaded with fruit recalled Jesus' parable of the barren fig tree and inspired him with desire to produce the fruit of good works. When he heard birds singing, he thought of heaven's new song. Even the sight of a donkey inspired him to prayerful thoughts!

St. Anthony also found engaging ways of sharing his thoughts in conversations aimed at bringing other people to Christ. Sometimes, he said, these chats had an effect similar to that of Jesus' conversation with the travelers to Emmaus (Lk 24:13-35)!

"I am afraid of the sea," said St. Frances Cabrini. You'd never know it from the many sea-inspired meditations in her letters, which she wrote during her ocean crossings. Obedience to her missionary calling enabled St. Frances to find material for prayer even in something she feared by nature.

Blessed voice of obedience! When that speaks, the missionary crosses the ocean and gives no thought to the roaring waters and the rising and falling of the billows. Then the ocean becomes to her a sublime and magnificent sight that overwhelms her with admiration, fills her heart with God, and leads her to praise the Creator for the beauty and wonder of his works.

During a rough period when she was treated as the family Cinderella, St. Catherine of Siena lovingly carried out her menial tasks with the help of a mental image.

In her imagination, she said, she vividly pictured her father as representing our Lord and Savior Jesus Christ; her mother as his most glorious Mother; her brothers and sisters and the rest of the household as his apostles and disciples. Picturing them in this fashion she was able to render them a cheerful and unfailing service which filled them with astonishment....

As she went about her tasks, she kept her mind fixed on her Spouse, regarding herself as in reality serving him. Outwardly she was in the kitchen; inwardly her soul was feasting on the presence of her Savior.

Blessed Raymond of Capua

Arrow Prayers

Blessed Marie of the Incarnation urged everyone to speak constantly to God by sending up short prayers to heaven. She herself acquired the habit from her mother, Marie told her sister in a 1645 letter:

I remember when our departed mother was alone at her work, she used to take advantage of her free time to make short, fervent prayers. At such times, I would hear her speaking to Our Lord about her children and her troubles. Perhaps you didn't notice it as much as I did, but you would be surprised at the impression it made on me.

A brief lifting up of the heart is enough. A brief remembrance of God, an act of inner adoration—even though on the run with sword in hand—these prayers, short as they may be, are pleasing to God.... There is nothing easier than to repeat these little inner adorations frequently throughout the day.

Brother Lawrence of the Resurrection

A good way to train ourselves to pray these short prayers is to go through the petitions of the Our Father one after another, choosing a sentence for each day. For example, today you have chosen "Our Father who art in heaven." Start by saying, "My Father, you who are in heaven." Fifteen minutes later, say, "If you are my Father, when shall I be completely your daughter?" And so you will continue on to another part of your prayer at each quarter-hour.

St. Francis de Sales

Pray Always

We must pray literally without ceasing—without ceasing—in every occurrence and enjoyment of our lives.

St. Elizabeth Seton

This encouragement to make the Jesus Prayer a part of oneself is from the Orthodox saint Gregory Palamas.

Let no one think, my brother Christians, that it is the duty only of priests and monks to pray without ceasing, and not of laypeople. No, no. It is the duty of all of us Christians to remain always in prayer....

Do not neglect the practice of this prayer.... This very name of our Lord Jesus Christ, constantly invoked by you, will help you to overcome all difficulties, and in the course of time you will become used to this practice and will taste how sweet is the name of the Lord. Then you will learn by experience that this practice is not impossible and not difficult but both possible and easy.

Whatever the object of my prayer,
I never pray or worship you in vain;
the very act of praying brings me rich reward.
Teach me then, Holy Spirit, to pray without ceasing,
that you may grant me to rejoice unceasingly in you.

William of St. Thierry

ELEVEN

ONE BIG PRAYER CHAIN:
THE COMMUNION OF SAINTS

Dorothy Day was introduced to the communion of saints by a Catholic friend when she was eight and growing up in a religiously indifferent family in Chicago. "Little Mary Harrington had told me of the saints and the Blessed Mother, and had so taken away all my fear of an awesome God and a vast and lonely heaven," she wrote of this discovery. Not for another twenty-two years would Dorothy be formally received into the Catholic Church. Still, the reality of the saints' friendship offered her hope, stirred her love, and developed into a distinguishing characteristic of her spiritual life, as well as a support for her demanding service of the needy through the Catholic Worker Movement.

The saints became real to Dorothy—"new companions to look forward to meeting some day." Their life stories drew her to Christ and gave her examples to imitate. Their writings guided her into deeper prayer. Their intercession became a source of strength. Early on, Dorothy read St. Thérèse of Lisieux's promise, "I will spend my heaven doing good on earth"; that made her feel "even closer to all the saints," she said. She was especially drawn to Thérèse, Catherine of Siena, Teresa of Avila, Francis of Assisi, St. Joseph, and the Blessed Mother.

But membership in the communion of saints involves more than being on the receiving end of prayers from heaven. It means interceding ourselves for the spiritual and material needs of other members of Christ's body on earth, as well as for those who are being purified in purgatory. Dorothy took this call seriously. Jim Forest, who worked with her at a hospitality house in a seedy section of Manhattan, reports: "One day, looking into the Bible and Missal she had left behind when summoned for a phone call, I found long lists of people, living and dead, whom she prayed for daily." In her *Catholic Worker* newspaper columns, Dorothy regularly invited readers to join her in praying for others, including deceased friends and acquaintances.

Dorothy Day isn't yet one of the Church's canonized saints; the process for her beatification and canonization was opened only in early 2000. But like the saints quoted in this chapter, Dorothy grasped the implications of belonging to a community that transcends time and even death, and whose members are called to mutual love and assistance. Both in our prayer and in our pursuit of the works of mercy, Dorothy Day shows us how to do the same.

Saints Reading Saints

It was a saying of St. Philip Neri that, both for study and for prayer, we should read chiefly "the authors whose names begin with S"—that is, the lives and writings of the saints.

St. Teresa of Avila read St. Augustine's Confessions *when she was emerging from years of "indulging in one pastime, one vanity, and one occasion of sin after another." She was drawn to Augustine, she said, partly because "he had been a sinner."*

I used to find a great deal of comfort in reading about the lives of saints who had been sinners before the Lord brought them back to himself. As he had forgiven them, I thought that he might do the same for me....

When I started to read the *Confessions,* I seemed to see myself in them and I began to commend myself often to this glorious saint. When I got as far as his conversion ..., it seemed exactly as if the Lord were speaking to me, or so my heart felt.

St. Edith Stein was searching when, in 1921, she came across St. Teresa of Avila's autobiography. She read it all night. "I ... did not stop until I reached the end. As I closed the book, I said, this is the truth." Then, over a period of time, she read St. Teresa's books aloud—"more as if she were praying them than reading them," observed one of Edith's Jewish friends. Edith was baptized into the Catholic Church on January 1, 1922.

I'm reading the life of St. Bernard ... and it interests me very much. What a magnificent figure this monk is!.... Despite our littleness, we can gain much through contact with people like this. They teach us to generously carry out the much more modest work that God asks of us in a simple, joyful, strong way—without looking at apparent results or at ourselves. Especially they teach us that suffering is the lot of Jesus' friends, that nothing great is accomplished without it, that it obtains all and digs the channel through which the great river of grace flows out to souls. Finally, the saints show us the infinite power of prayer and its hidden action.

Elisabeth Leseur

When St. Ignatius of Loyola began reading the lives of the saints,
he didn't have the slightest desire for high holiness. There were just
no other books in the house where he was convalescing from a leg
injury! Speaking of himself in the third person, he describes how
grace overtook him as he read:

> While reading the life of our Lord and those of the saints
> he used to pause and meditate, reasoning with himself:
> "What if I were to do what St. Francis did, or to do what
> St. Dominic did?"... He used to say to himself: "St.
> Dominic did this, so I have to do it too. St. Francis did
> this, so I have to do it too."...
>
> He began to think more seriously about his past life and
> how greatly he needed to do penance for it. It was at this
> time that the desire to imitate the saints came to him, and
> without giving any consideration to his present circum-
> stances, he promised to do, with God's grace, what they
> had done.

> Right now at our meetings [of the St. Vincent de Paul
> Society, which Ozanam founded], we're reading the life of
> St. Vincent de Paul ... so that his example and traditions
> will sink more deeply into us. Indeed, a holy patron isn't a
> meaningless figurehead for an organization.... He's a
> model we must strive to take on for ourselves, just as he
> himself took on the divine model, Jesus Christ. We must
> continue this patron's life, warm our hearts in his, seek
> inspiration from his thinking.

> *Blessed Frederic Ozanam*

St. Anthony Mary Claret called St. Catherine of Siena "my teacher and my guide." He declared himself so moved by her biography that he always read it with "the book in one hand and a handkerchief in the other, to dry the tears it causes." St. Teresa of Avila was another special guide: on two occasions, in 1864 and 1869, Anthony received deep insights as he read her works. No surprise that he chose St. Catherine and St. Teresa as co-patrons of his Congregation of Missionaries.

Saints Praying to Saints

For if it is lawful and profitable to invoke living saints to aid us, and to beseech them to assist us in prayers, as the prophet Baruch did—"And pray for us to the Lord our God" (Bar 1:13)—and St. Paul—"Brethren, pray for us" (1 Thes 5:25)—and as God himself commanded the friends of Job—"Go to my servant Job,... and my servant Job shall pray for you" (Jb 42:8)—if then it is lawful to recommend ourselves to the living, how can it be unlawful to invoke the saints who in heaven enjoy God face to face? This is not derogatory to the honor due to God, but it is doubling it; for it is honoring the king not only in his person but in his servants.

St. Alphonsus Liguori

St. Elizabeth Ann Seton's children had heard Catholics pray the Hail Mary and wanted their mother to teach it to them. Elizabeth, still an Episcopalian, finally concluded, Why not?

And I ask my Savior why we should not say it. If any one is in heaven, his mother must be there. Are the angels, then, who are so often represented as being entrusted for us on earth, more compassionate or more exalted than she is? Oh! no, no, Mary our Mother, that cannot be! So I beseech her with the confidence and tenderness of her child to pity us and guide us to the true faith.... I kiss her picture ... and beg her to be a mother to us.

I took for my advocate and lord the glorious St. Joseph and commended myself earnestly to him....

I wish I could persuade everyone to be devoted to this glorious saint, for I have great experience of the blessings which he can obtain from God. I have never known anyone to be truly devoted to him .... who did not notably advance in virtue, for he gives very real help to souls who commend themselves to him....

I only beg, for the love of God, that anyone who does not believe me will put what I say to the test, and he will see by experience what great advantages come from his commending himself to this glorious patriarch and having devotion to him. Those who practice prayer should have a special affection for him always.... If anyone cannot find a master to teach him how to pray, let him take this glorious saint as his master and he will not go astray.

St. Teresa of Avila

Long before he had any suspicion that he would become Pope John XXIII, Angelo Roncalli felt drawn to St. Francis de Sales for his gentle goodness. If only he could be like this saintly bishop of Geneva, he once wrote, he wouldn't even mind "if they were to make me pope!" The same journal entry, written on the feast of St. Francis, ends with this heartfelt request to his heavenly patron:

O my loving saint, as I kneel before you at this moment, there is so much I could say to you! I love you tenderly and I will always remember you and look to you for help. O St. Francis, I can say no more; you can see into my heart, give me what I need to become like you.

Imagine yourselves to be spiritual beggars in the presence of God and his saints. You should go round from saint to saint, imploring an alms with the same earnestness with which the poor beg.

St. Philip Neri

Praying for Others

Prayer. In my opinion, this is the greatest means that can be used for the conversion of sinners, the perseverance of the just, and the relief of the souls in purgatory.

St. Anthony Mary Claret

We must also turn to prayer so that we may place the needs of [others] ... before our Lord. It is quite clear that we shall gain more results by this means than by any other. Jesus Christ—who should be our guide in all things—did not think it sufficient to preach, labor, fast, and die for us. He also prayed. Not that he needed prayers for himself. It was for us that he prayed so continually—and also to teach us to pray for ourselves and for those he is helping us to lead to him.

St. Vincent de Paul

Beset by illness for much of her life, Elisabeth Leseur felt drawn to intercessory prayer—for souls in purgatory, the dying, priests, and especially for "God's conquest of the souls I love, ... my husband, my mother, my dear nephews and niece, my sister, all the dear relations, and other people as well.... That is the object of my life."

Elisabeth loved the Feasts of All Saints and All Souls—days when, as it seemed to her, the communion of saints made itself felt as a "more active, more tender" reality. She considered the communion of saints "one of the greatest joys of the spiritual life." One reason: "For those who, like myself, are almost useless to all outward appearances, it is very sweet to think that in God's hands, sufferings and sacrifices become active and beneficial, and that, passing through the heart of Jesus, they are transformed into graces for others."

Though she never flattered herself that her prayers had special power, Elisabeth knew they were effective: "I believe in them because I believe in that divine, mysterious law we call the communion of saints. I know that no cry, no desire, no call proceeding from the depths of our soul, is lost; all go to God, and through him to those who moved us to pray. I know that only God performs the intimate transformation of a soul and that we can but point out to him those we love, saying, 'Lord, make them live.'"

Elisabeth had a premonition that her most cherished prayer—for the conversion of her husband, Felix—would be answered only after her death. This happened when Felix discovered her prayer journal and began a journey that led him into the Church and the priesthood.

> I consider the loss of faith the greatest disaster and the greatest unhappiness. How can one help grieving over friends and relatives and how insistent should be our prayers? We should be importunate as the friend trying to borrow some bread to feed his late guests, as the importunate widow before the unjust judge. But obedience to the command "Search the Scriptures" will give us the reassurance we need. Will a father, when he is asked for bread, give his son a stone?
>
> *Dorothy Day*

Only seven when Our Lady of Fatima appeared to her and two other children, Blessed Jacinta Marto was profoundly impressed by Mary's words about the seriousness of sin and by a vision of hell. The little girl decided to offer herself completely for the salvation of others. She prayed and took on many sacrifices— everything from giving away her snacks to enduring painful illness and a lonely hospital death just before her eleventh birthday.

"If only I could show hell to sinners! How happy I would be if all could go to paradise," Jacinta used to say. And, "If only I could place in the heart of everyone the fire I have in my heart which makes me love the heart of Mary so much!"

Two powerful visions of a suffering pontiff drew Jacinta to special intercession for the pope. "Poor Holy Father," said Jacinta, "there is a great need to pray for him."

On May 13, 2000, Pope John Paul II beatified Jacinta and her brother Francisco and acknowledged the girl's prayers. "I would like to celebrate the Lord's goodness to me when I was saved from death after being gravely wounded on 13 May 1981," said the Pope. "I also express my gratitude to Blessed Jacinta for the sacrifices and prayers offered for the Holy Father, whom she saw suffering greatly."

Almighty and tender Lord Jesus Christ,
I have asked you to be good to my friends,
and now I bring before you what I desire in my heart for
my enemies....
You who are the true light, lighten their darkness;
you who are the whole truth, correct their errors;
you who are the true life, give life to their souls.
For you have said to your beloved disciple
that he who loves not remains dead.
So I pray, Lord, that you will give them love for you
and love for their neighbor....
I have prayed as a weak man and a sinner;
you who are mighty and merciful, hear my prayer.

St. Anselm

Never cease offering me the incense of fragrant prayers for the salvation of souls, for I want to be merciful to the world. With your prayers and sweat and tears I will wash the face of my bride, holy Church.

St. Catherine of Siena

TWELVE

IT'S ALL ABOUT LOVE

Rome, 1544. Alone in the catacombs, where he often keeps night vigils, a twenty-nine-year-old layman is praying earnestly to the Holy Spirit. Asking for the Spirit's gifts and graces has become a daily habit with him, but tonight, thoughts of the approaching feast of Pentecost stir him to special fervor. His prayer is answered in a sudden, unusual way: a globe of fire enters his mouth, setting his heart aflame with love. It is Philip Neri's personal Pentecost.

The effects of this encounter with God stayed with St. Philip for the rest of his long life. A large swelling formed over his heart, which from then on beat violently and radiated tremendous heat. (An autopsy after his death revealed an enlarged heart; over it, two broken ribs served as a protective arch.)

After this, Philip's whole life, which had been mainly solitary, became centered on leading others to encounter God's love for them. Literally burning with the fire of love, Philip often communicated it with a simple hug; on many occasions, the sick or the sinful were healed as he pulled them to himself. Ordained a priest in 1551, he began an apostolate of the confessional, where his tenderness and gift of reading hearts led thousands to repentance. He invited people over for informal sessions of prayer and discussion centered on Scripture. On these occasions, Philip spoke from the heart, letting the Spirit guide his reflections on the biblical text. People came away stirred by God's love. Eventually, Philip had a converting effect on the whole city of Rome—all because, in meeting him, people met Jesus.

Saints like Philip Neri reveal something of the ultimate effect of prayer, which is union with God through transformation in Christ. St. Paul pointed to the same reality: "I live, no longer I, but Christ who lives in me" (Gal 2:20).

Dynamic, radiant love that transforms us and overflows to others—if we pray, this is the goal toward which God moves us. Most of us will be struck by the discrepancy between ourselves and this chapter's descriptions of that love and its effects. Still, as we persevere and put our trust in God, he will do for us what he did for the saints. This story from the Desert Fathers—an apt commentary on Philip Neri's life—encourages us not to expect too little:

Abbot Lot came to Abbot Joseph and said: Father, according as I am able, I keep my little rule, and my little fast, my prayer, meditation, and contemplative silence.... What more should I do? The elder rose up in reply and stretched out his hands to heaven, and his fingers became like ten lamps of fire. He said: Why not be totally changed into fire?

The Delights of Loving God in Prayer

As the saints drew near to God, they experienced—and often eloquently expressed—the joy of all-consuming love.

While I was about to go to Holy Communion, I seemed to be thrown wide open like a door flung open to welcome a close friend and then shut tight after his entry. So my heart was alone with him—alone with God. It seems impossible to relate all the effects, feelings, leaping delight, and festivity my soul experienced.

If I were to speak, for example, of all the happy and pleasant times shared with dear friends..., I would be saying nothing comparable to this joy. And if I were to add up all the occasions of rejoicing in the universe, I would be saying that all this amounts to little or nothing beside what, in an instant, my heart experiences in the presence of God. Or rather what God does to my heart, because all these other things flow from him and are his works.

Love makes the heart leap and dance. Love makes it exult and be festive. Love makes it sing and be silent as it pleases. Love grants it rest and enables it to act. Love possesses it and gives it everything. Loves takes it over completely and dwells in it. But I am unable to say more because if I wished to relate all the effects that my heart experiences in the act of going to Holy Communion and also at other times, I would never finish saying everything. It is sufficient to say that Communion is a ... mansion of love itself.

St. Veronica Giuliani

To love Jesus is a wondrous thing.... There is nothing sweeter than love, nothing stronger, nothing higher, nothing wider, nothing fuller, nothing better in heaven or earth; for love is born of God, and only in God, above all that he has created, can it find rest.

A man in love treads on air; he runs for very joy. He is a free man; nothing can hold him back.... Love often knows no limits; its impetuous fire leaps across every boundary. Love feels no burden, makes light of every toil, strives for things beyond its strength....

Love is ever on the watch; it rests, but does not slumber, is wearied but not spent.... Like a living flame, a blazing torch, it shoots upward.... A loud cry in the ears of God is that burning love for him in the soul which says: "My God, my love, you are all mine and I am all yours."

Thomas à Kempis

O infinite goodness of my God!... O Joy of the angels! When I consider it, I wish I could wholly die of love! How true it is that you bear with those who will not bear you! Oh, how good a friend you are, my Lord! How you comfort and endure and also wait for us to become more like you, and yet in the meantime you are so patient of the state we are in! You take into account the occasions when we seek you, and when we do penance for a moment, you forget our offenses against you.

I have seen this distinctly in my own case, and I cannot understand why the whole world does not labor to draw near to you in this special friendship. Those of us who are wicked, who do not resemble you, ought to do so in order that you may make them good. For that purpose, they should allow you to remain with them at least for two hours daily, even though they may not remain with you but, as I used to do, with a thousand distractions and with worldly thoughts. In return, ... you, O Lord, defend them against the assaults of evil spirits, whose power you restrain and even lessen daily, giving them the victory over these enemies. So it is, O Life of all lives, you slay none that put their trust in you and seek your friendship; rather, you sustain their bodily life in greater vigor and make their soul live.

St. Teresa of Avila

Becoming What We Contemplate

We cannot see Christ and remain as we are. We cannot exchange a look with Christ and not be overcome with a total conversion. If we are still tepid and still attached to our ease ... it is because we have not exchanged glances with Christ; we have not really "seen" Christ.

Père Jacques (Lucien-Louis Bunel)

Continual, humble prayer has a truly amazing outcome, says St. Catherine of Siena.

By such prayer the soul is united with God, following in the footsteps of Christ crucified, and through desire and affection and the union of love he makes of her another himself.

Prayer is the key to understanding and experiencing the depths of meaning suggested by Jesus' words, "Abide in me" (Jn 15:4).

"Abide in me": not for a few moments, a few passing hours, but abide permanently, habitually. Abide in me, pray in me, adore in me, love in me, suffer in me, work in me, act in me. Abide in me, whatever the person or action you are concerned with, penetrating ever deeper into this abode.... But to grasp the meaning of this mysterious appeal we must do more than listen to it superficially; we must immerse ourselves deeply, and more deeply still, into the Divinity by means of recollection. "I follow after," exclaimed St. Paul (Phil 3:12). So should we descend daily by this path into the abyss, which is God himself.... It is there ... that the abyss of our nothingness will find itself face to face with the abyss of the mercy, with the immensity of the All of God. There shall we find the strength to die to self and, losing all trace of self, we shall be transformed in love. "Blessed are they who die in the Lord" (Rv 14:13).

Blessed Elizabeth of the Trinity

We follow him and he draws us to himself by love.... Prayer makes the soul one with God.

Julian of Norwich

Place your mind before the mirror of eternity!
Place your soul in the brilliance of glory!
Place your heart in the figure of the divine substance!
And transform your whole being into the image
of the Godhead Itself through contemplation!
So that you too may feel what his friends feel

as they taste the hidden sweetness
which God himself has reserved
from the beginning for those who love him.

> *St. Clare of Assisi*

Pray, Love, Reach Out

Watch yourself to make sure there's a good fit between your praying and your living, warns St. John Vianney.

Night and morning you fold your hands and say in prayer, "My God, I love you with my whole heart and above all things." And when praying like this, you believe that you are speaking the truth. And yet a few hours after, your hand may be busy injuring your neighbor; your mouth, which has expressed your love of God will, perhaps, be soiled with oaths, tale-bearing, calumnies, and all sorts of slander, thus dishonoring and abusing that same God to whom you have just said that you love him with your whole heart. Do your actions prove your words?

Don't be thrown out of the heavenly banquet, says St. Augustine. Put on "the wedding garment of charity" that will let you in (see Mt 22:1-14).

Extend your love, and not only as far as your husbands, wives, and children. That degree of love is to be found even among cattle and sparrows.... But extend your love, let this love grow.... First love God. Extend yourselves toward God, and grab whom you can for God. An enemy, perhaps; have him snatched for God. A son, a wife, a slave, have them snatched off to God. A stranger perhaps; have him snatched off to God. Grab, grab your enemy; by being grabbed he will cease to be your enemy.

That's the way we should be making progress: that's the way charity should be nourished and eventually brought to perfection. That's how the wedding garment should be put on. That's how the image of God to which we were created should be progressively sculpted afresh.

When I see people very diligently trying to discover what type of prayer they are experiencing and so completely wrapped up in their prayers that they seem afraid to stir, or to indulge in a moment's thought, lest they should lose the slightest degree of the tenderness and devotion which they have been feeling, I realize how little they understand of the road to the attainment of union. They think that the whole thing consists in this. But no, sisters, no; what the Lord desires is works. If you see a sick woman to whom you can give some help, never be affected by the fear that your devotion will suffer, but take pity on her; if she is in pain, you should feel pain too; if necessary, fast so that she may have your food, not so much for her sake as because you know it to be your Lord's will. That is true union with his will.

St. Teresa of Avila

When I began to taste God in prayer and in the reception of the most Blessed Sacrament, my heart was set on fire more intensely and I was moved with pity and compassion towards the poor. I was kind toward everyone, and I tried to take care of everyone's needs without considering that thereby I would have to do without something myself. Our Lord joined faith and hope to my charity, and I firmly believed and trusted that he would be my sure provider.

St. Charles of Sezze

We have been sent here not only to love God ourselves, but to make others love him. It is not enough for us to love God if our neighbor does not love him also; and we cannot be loving our neighbor as ourselves unless we achieve for him the blessing that is our great object for ourselves: that is to say, the perfect love which unites us with God, our Supreme Good. We must love our neighbor, as being made in the image of God and as an object of his love....

If we have one spark of that sacred fire that glowed in the heart of Jesus Christ, can we remain with folded hands? Can we neglect those whom we might be helping? Not at all, because real charity cannot stand idle nor allow us to see our friends in need without showing them our love.

St. Vincent de Paul

Prayer is powerful! It fills the earth with mercy.... The mercy and clemency obtained through the power of prayer will always produce its generous and saving effects in people. The mercy obtained through prayer will be like a torrent coming from that immense ocean of the inexhaustible goodness of the adorable heart of Jesus. It will ... quietly dispose those people to approach God and enter into the ark of eternal salvation.

St. Frances Cabrini

Praying for Love

O God, love, who have created me, recreate me in your
love.
O love, who have redeemed me,
whatever I have neglected of your love,
amend for yourself and redeem in me.
O God, love, who with the blood of your
Christ have ransomed me for yourself,
sanctify me in your truth....
grant that I may cherish you
with all my heart, all my soul, all my strength....
O love, almighty God, embolden me in your love.
[O] wisest love, grant that I may love you wisely....

St. Gertrude the Great

Give me the grace, my Jesus, to love you out of love and
not fear.

St. Philip Neri

O you who have willed to be called charity, give me charity, that I may love you more than I love myself, not car-
ing at all what I do with myself, so long as I am doing what
is pleasing in your sight. Grant me, O Father—though I
dare not always call myself your child—grant me at least to
be your faithful little servant and the sheep of your pasture.
Speak to your servant's heart sometimes, O Lord, so that
your consolations may give joy to my soul (Ps 93:19). And
teach me to speak to you often in prayer.

William of St. Thierry

Saints' Biographies

St. Albert the Great (1206–280); German; Dominican; philosopher, theologian, scientist; bishop; Doctor of the Church

Bl. Alphonsus de Orozco (1500–1591); Spanish; Augustinian; prior, preacher, spiritual writer

St. Alphonsus Liguori (1696–1787); Italian; founder of Redemptorists; missionary, reformer, spiritual writer; bishop; Doctor of the Church

Bl. André Bessette (1845–1937); French Canadian; Holy Cross brother and porter; known for healing ministry, devotion to St. Joseph, and foundation of the Oratory of St. Joseph, in Montreal

St. Angela Merici (1470?–1540); Italian; educator; foundress of the Ursulines

St. Anselm (1033–1109); Italian; monk, archbishop, political activist, theologian; Doctor of the Church

St. Anthony the Great (251–356); Egyptian; hermit, ascetic, a founder of monasticism

St. Anthony Mary Claret (1807–70); Spanish; founder of Claretians; writer, preacher, reformer, missionary; archbishop of Santiago, Cuba

St. Augustine of Hippo (354–430); African; preacher, writer, theologian; bishop; Father and Doctor of the Church

St. Bernadette Soubirous (1844–79); French; recipient of eighteen apparitions of Our Lady at Lourdes; spent the rest of her life in the Sisters of Notre Dame of Nevers

St. Bernard of Clairvaux (1090?–1153); French; Cistercian abbot; reformer, preacher, theologian, writer, political figure; Doctor of the Church

St. Bonaventure (1218?–74); Italian; Franciscan; theologian, philosopher, spiritual writer; Doctor of the Church

St. Catherine of Siena (1347–80); Italian; evangelizer, political and spiritual advisor, servant of the poor, mystic; Doctor of the Church

Ven. Charles de Foucauld (1858–1916); French; priest, hermit, "little brother of Jesus," whose plan for prayer, evangelistic witness, and service to the poor inspired five religious congregations; murdered in Algeria

St. Charles of Sezze (1613–70); Italian; Franciscan; mystic, spiritual counselor and writer

St. Clare of Assisi (1193–1253); Italian; cofounder of the Poor Clares; abbess, mystic, influential counselor

St. Claude La Colombière (1642–82); French; Jesuit; preacher, writer, spiritual director of St. Margaret Mary Alacoque

Bl. Columba Marmion (1858–1923); Irish; Benedictine abbot, writer, spiritual director

St. Dominic (1170–1221); Spanish; Scripture scholar and theologian; reformer, evangelizer, contemplative, founder of the order of Friars Preachers (Dominicans)

Dorothy Day, Servant of God (1897–1980); American; peace and social justice activist; writer; cofounder of the Catholic Worker Movement

St. Edith Stein (Teresa Benedicta of the Cross) (1891–1924); German; Jewish philosopher, educator, writer; Carmelite nun; murdered at Auschwitz

Elisabeth Leseur, Servant of God (1866–1914); French; wife, intercessor, contemplative, exemplar of redemptive suffering

St. Elizabeth Ann Seton (1774–1821); American; wife, mother, widow; foundress of the Sisters of Charity; first U.S.-born saint to be canonized

Bl. Elizabeth of the Trinity (1880–1906); French; Carmelite nun; mystic, spiritual writer

St. Ephrem (306?–73?); Syrian; hermit; deacon; Scripture scholar, writer, poet, composer of hymns; Doctor of the Church

Evagrius (346–99); Egyptian; preacher, spiritual guide, one of the first Desert Fathers to write about the spiritual life

St. Frances Cabrini (1850–1917); Italian; foundress of Missionary Sisters of the Sacred Heart and of many hospitals, schools, orphanages; known for work with Italian immigrants in the U.S.; first canonized U.S. citizen

St. Francis of Assisi (1181–1226); Italian; founder of Order of Friars Minor (Franciscans), Third Order; cofounder of Poor Clares; lover of poverty; missionary, mystic, stigmatist

St. Francis de Sales (1567–1622); French; cofounder of the Order of the Visitation; missionary, spiritual writer; bishop; Doctor of the Church

Bl. Frederic Ozanam (1813–53); French; husband, father; lawyer, scholar, writer, literature professor; founder of the St. Vincent de Paul Society

St. Gertrude the Great (1256–1302); German; Benedictine nun; Scripture scholar, writer, mystic, visionary

Gilbert of Hoyland (d. 1172); Dutch; Cistercian abbot; preacher, spiritual writer

St. Gregory Palamas (1296–1359); Greek; monk, archbishop, spiritual teacher and writer

St. Gregory of Sinai (d. 1346); Cypriot; monk on Mounts Sinai, Athos; master and teacher of contemplative prayer, especially the Jesus Prayer

Bl. Henry Suso (1298?–1366); Swiss; Dominican preacher, teacher, spiritual writer and director, mystic

St. Ignatius of Loyola (1491–1556); Spanish; founder of the Society of Jesus (Jesuits); reformer, spiritual director, author of *Spiritual Exercises*

St. Isaac of Syria (d. end of sixth century); Syrian; monk, bishop, spiritual writer

Bl. Jacinta Marto (1910–20); Portuguese; one of the three children to whom Our Lady appeared at Fatima

St. Jane Frances de Chantal (1572–1641); French; wife, mother, widow; cofounder of the Order of the Visitation; spiritual director and writer

Bl. Jeanne Jugan (1792–1879); French; main foundress of the Little Sisters of the Poor, providing special care for the elderly

St. Jerome (341?–420); born in Dalmatia; priest, hermit, monastery founder; translator and commentator of Scripture; Doctor of the Church

Bl. John XXIII (1881–1963); Italian; priest, Vatican diplomat, pope; convened Second Vatican Council in 1962

St. John Cassian (360?–433?); Romanian; priest, monk, monastic father and writer

St. John Damascene (675?–749?); Greek; monk, theologian, composer; Father of the Church

St. John Chrysostom (347–407); Greek; monk, priest, eloquent preacher; patriarch of Constantinople

St. John Climacus (579?–649?); Palestinian; desert monk and hermit; abbot, influential author

St. John of the Cross (1542–91); Spanish; Carmelite priest and coworker of St. Teresa of Avila; poet, mystic, classic spiritual writer

St. John Gabriel Perboyre (1802–40); French; Vincentian priest; missionary to China; martyr

Ven. John Henry Newman (1801–90); English; Anglican convert to Catholicism; scholar, teacher, writer, cardinal

St. John Vianney, the Curé of Ars (1786–1859); French; model parish priest and saintly confessor with a gift of physical and spiritual healing

Bl. Josemaría Escrivá de Balaguer (1902–75); Spanish; priest; founder of Opus Dei

Julian of Norwich (1342?–1423?); English; recluse, mystic, spiritual writer

Lawrence of the Resurrection (1605?–91); French; Carmelite brother; cook, gardener, contemplative, teacher of prayer

St. Louise de Marillac (1591–1660); French; wife, mother, widow; cofounder of Sisters of Charity

Lucien-Louis Bunel (Père Jacques), Servant of God (1900–45); French; Carmelite priest, teacher; thrown into Mauthausen concentration camp for opposing the Nazis and sheltering three Jewish boys

St. Macarius the Great (300?–90); Egyptian; hermit, Desert Father, founder of influential colony of monks

Bl. Marie of the Incarnation (1599–1672); French; wife, mother, widow; Ursuline nun, mystic, missionary to Canada

St. Mark the Ascetic (fourth century); Egyptian; Desert Father, spiritual director, writer

St. Mary Euphrasia Pelletier (1796–1868); French; worked with ex-prostitutes and homeless, delinquent girls; founded the Good Shepherd Sisters

St. Nilus of Sinai (d. 450); Greek; monk, Desert Father, spiritual master and writer

St. Paul of the Cross (1694–1775); Italian; founder of the Passionists; missionary, preacher, spiritual director

St. Peter of Alcantara (1499–1562); Spanish; Franciscan; founder of the Alcantarines; reformer, spiritual director

St. Peter Chrysologus (406–50?); Italian; preacher, reformer; archbishop; Doctor of the Church

St. Peter Julian Eymard (1811–68); French; priest; founder of two religious orders and several organizations devoted to adoration of the Blessed Sacrament

St. Philip Neri (1515–95); Italian; priest, founder of the Congregation of the Oratory; mystic and evangelizer

Bl. Raymond of Capua (1333–99); Italian; Dominican priest; spiritual director and biographer of St. Catherine of Siena

Ven. Solanus Casey (1870–1957); American; Capuchin Franciscan; porter, spiritual counselor with a healing ministry

St. Teresa of Avila (1515–82); Spanish; Carmelite nun; reformer, writer, teacher of prayer; Doctor of the Church

St. Thérèse of Lisieux (1873–97); French; Carmelite nun; teacher of prayer; Doctor of the Church

Thomas à Kempis (1379?–1471); Dutch; Augustinian canon; preacher, spiritual director, wrote *The Imitation of Christ*

St. Thomas Aquinas (1225–74); Italian; Dominican theologian, philosopher, teacher, writer; Doctor of the Church

St. Thomas More (1477–1535); English; husband, father; scholar, humanist, chancellor of England; beheaded for refusing to acknowledge King Henry VIII as head of the church in England

Bl. Titus Brandsma (1881–1942); Dutch; Carmelite priest; philosophy professor, writer, friend to the poor; killed at Dachau

St. Veronica Giuliani (1660–1727); Italian; Capuchin abbess; spiritual writer, mystic, stigmatist, visionary

St. Vincent de Paul (1581–1660); French; founder of the Congregation of the Mission for priests; cofounder of the Sisters of Charity; organizer of many outreaches to the poor, sick, and suffering

William of St. Thierry (1085?–d. after 1135); Belgian; Benedictine monk, abbot, friend of St. Bernard; reformer, mystic, spiritual writer

Sources

Alphonsus Liguori
The Great Means of Salvation and Perfection. Trans. E. Grimm. New York, Cincinnati, St. Louis: Benziger, 1886.

Alphonsus de Orozco
Pond, K. *The Spirit of the Spanish Mystics.* London: Burns & Oates, 1958.

André Bessette
Bergeron, H. *The Wonder Man of Mount Royal.* Trans. R. Boudreau. Montreal: Fides, 1958.

Angela Merici
Monica, Sr. M. *Angela Merici and Her Teaching Idea.* New York, London: Longmans, Green, and Co., 1927.

Anselm
The Prayers and Meditations of St. Anselm. Trans. B. Ward, New York: Penguin, 1973.

Anthony Mary Claret
Autobiography. Trans. J. Vinas.Chicago: Claretian, 1976.

Augustine
The Confessions. Trans. M. Boulding. Hyde Park, N.Y.: New City, 1997.
Pope, H. *The Teaching of St. Augustine on Prayer and the Contemplative Life.* London: Burns, Oates & Washbourne, 1935.
The Works of St. Augustine Vol. 3. Trans. E. Hill.Hyde Park, N.Y.: New City, 1992.
Groeschel, B. *Augustine. Major Writings.* New York: Crossroad, 1996.

Bernadette Soubirous
Trochu, F. *Saint Bernadette Soubirous.* Trans. J. Joyce. Rockford, Ill.: Tan, 1985.

Bernard of Clairvaux

Saint Bernard on the Song of Songs. Trans. Religious of CSMV. London: Mowbray, 1952.

St. Bernard's Sermons for the Seasons and Principal Festivals of the Year. Priest of Mount Melleray, trans. Westminster, Md.: Carroll Press, 1925.

The Works of Bernard of Clairvaux Vol. 2: On the Song of Songs I. Trans. K. Walsh. Kalamazoo, Mich.: Cistercian, 1981.

The Works of Bernard of Clairvaux Vol. 3: On the Song of Songs II. Trans. K. Walsh. Kalamazoo, Mich.: Cistercian, 1979.

Catherine of Siena

The Dialogue. Trans. S. Noffke.New York: Paulist, 1980.

Charles de Foucauld

Spiritual Meditations on Faith. Trans. A. Russell. New York: New City, 1988.

Spiritual Autobiography of Charles de Foucauld. Ed. J.-F. Six. Trans. J.H. Smith. Denville, N.J.: Dimension, 1964.

Charles of Sezze

Autobiography. Trans. L. Perotti. London: Catholic Book Club, 1963.

Clare of Assisi

Francis and Clare, The Complete Works. New York: Paulist, 1982.

Claude la Colombière

Guitton, G. *Perfect Friend, the Life of Blessed Claude La Colombière, S.J.* St. Louis and London: Herder, 1956.

The Spiritual Direction of Saint Claude de la Colombière. Trans. Mother M. Philip. San Francisco: Ignatius, 1998.

Columba Marmion

The English Letters of Columba Marmion, 1858-1923. Ed. G. Ghysens and T. Delforge. Baltimore, Dublin: Helicon, 1962.

Christ, the Ideal of the Monk. St. Louis: Herder, 1926.

Christ, the Ideal of the Priest. St. Louis: Herder, 1928.
Christ in His Mysteries. St. Louis: Herder, 1924.
Dollen, C. *Fire of Love.* St. Louis: Herder, 1964.

Dominic
Lehner, F. *Saint Dominic: Biographical Documents.* Washington, D.C.: Thomist, 1964.

Dorothy Day
Dorothy Day Library on the Web at www.catholicworker.org.
O'Shea Merriman, B. *Searching for Christ: The Spirituality of Dorothy Day.* Notre Dame, Ind.: Notre Dame, 1994.

Edith Stein
The Collected Works of Edith Stein. Vol. 2, Essays on Woman. Trans. F. Oben. Washington, D.C.: ICS Publications, 1987.
Herbstrith, W. *Edith Stein: A Biography.* San Francisco: Harper & Row, 1971.

Elisabeth Leseur
A Wife's Story, The Journal of Elizabeth Leseur. London: Burns, Oates & Washbourne, 1921.
Lettres sur la souffrance. Ed. F. Leseur. Paris: J. de Gigord, 1927.

Elizabeth Ann Seton
A Daily Thought from the Writings of Mother Seton. Ed. J. Code. Emmitsburg, Md.: Sisters of Charity, 1929.
A Daughter of Charity. *The Soul of Elizabeth Seton.* New York, Cincinnati, Chicago, San Francisco: Benziger, 1936.
Dirvin, J. *Mrs. Seton: Foundress of the American Sisters of Charity.* New York: Farrar, Straus, and Giroux, 1962.
Feeney, L. *Mother Seton. Saint Elizabeth of New York.* Cambridge, Mass.: Ravengate, 1975.
Sadlier, A. *Elizabeth Seton: Her Life and Work.* Philadelphia: H.L. Kilner, 1905.

Elizabeth of the Trinity

I Have Found God: Letters from Carmel, in *Complete Works* Vol. 2.
　　Trans. A. Englund North.Washington, D.C.: ICS, 1995.

Philipon, M.M. *The Spiritual Doctrine of Sister Elizabeth of the
　　Trinity*. Trans. A Benedictine of Stanbrook Abbey. Westminster,
　　Md.: Newman, 1947.

Ephrem

St. Ephrem the Syrian, Hymns on Paradise. Trans. S. Brock.
　　Crestwood, N.Y.: St. Vladimir's Seminary, 1990.

Francis of Assisi

Jorgensen, J. *Francis of Assisi*. New York, London, Toronto:
　　Longmans, Green, 1912.

Writings and Early Biographies: English Omnibus of Sources.
　　Ed. M. Habig. Chicago: Franciscan, 1983.

Frances Xavier Cabrini

*The Travels of Mother Frances Xavier Cabrini, as related in several of
　　her letters*. Exeter: Giovanni Serpentilli, 1925.

Francis de Sales

Francis de Sales and Jane de Chantal: Letters of Spiritual Direction.
　　Trans. P. Thibert. Mahwah, N.J.: Paulist, 1988.

Introduction to the Devout Life. Trans. A. Nazareth, A. Mookenthottam,
　　A. Kolencherry. Bangalore, India: S.F.S., 1990.

Library of St. Francis de Sales. Vols. 1, 4, 5. Trans. H. B. Mackey.
　　London: Burns, Oates, & Washbourne, 1873–1910.

Selected Letters. Trans. E. Stopp. London: Faber & Faber/ New
　　York: Harper and Bros., 1960.

The Sermons of St. Francis de Sales 1: On Prayer. Ed. L. Fiorelli. F.
　　Leary, trans. Rockford, Ill.: TAN, 1985.

Treatise on the Love of God. Trans. H. B. Mackey.Westminster, Md.:
　　Newman Bookshop, 1942.

The Love of God, a Treatise. Trans. V. Kerns.Westminster, Md.:
　　Newman Press, 1962.

Frederic Ozanam

Oeuvres complètes de Frederic Ozanam. Vols. 10–11. Paris, Lyons:
  Jacques Lecoffre, 1865.
O'Meara, K. *Life and Works of Frederic Ozanam.* New York:
  Catholic Truth, 1883.

Gertrude the Great

Spiritual Exercises. Trans. G. Lewis and Jack Lewis.Kalamazoo,
  Mich.: Cistercian, 1989.

Gilbert of Hoyland

In the School of Love: An Anthology of Early Cistercian Texts.
  Ed. E. Scholl. Kalamazoo, Mich.: Cistercian, 2000.

Henry Suso

Henry Suso: The Exemplar and Two German Sermons. New York:
  Paulist, 1989.
The Sister's Guide: The Letters of Henry Suso. Trans. K. Goldmann.
  Springfield, Ill.: Templegate, 1955.

Ignatius of Loyola

A Pilgrim's Journey. Autobiography of Ignatius of Loyola. Ed. and
  Trans. J. Tylenda. Collegeville, Minn.: Liturgical/Michael
  Glazier, 1985.
The Spiritual Exercises of Saint Ignatius. Trans. D. Fleming.
  St. Louis: Institute of Jesuit Sources, 1978.
The Spiritual Exercises of St. Ignatius. Trans. A. Mottola. Garden
  City, N.Y.: Doubleday Image, 1964.

Jane Frances de Chantal

St. Chantal on Prayer. Trans. A. Durand. Boston: St. Paul, 1968.
Selected Letters of St. Jane Frances de Chantal. Trans. Sisters of the
  Visitation.Harrow-on-the-Hill, London: Washbourne & Oates, 1918.
*St. Jane Frances Frémyot de Chantal: Her Exhortations, Conferences
  and Instructions. Trans.* Bristol Sisters of the Visitation.
  Westminster, Md.: The Newman Bookshop, 1947.

Stopp, E. *Madame de Chantal: Portrait of a Saint.* Westminster, Md.: Newman, 1963.

Jeanne Jugan
Milcent, P. *Fondatrice des Petites Soeurs des Pauvres.* Online at http://perso.wanadoo.fr/jmjtkern/jm.

John Cassian
Conferences. Trans. C. Luibheid. New York: Paulist, 1985.

John Chrysostom
Migne. *Patrologiae Graecae* 48, 991-93. "Homily 3, on Lazarus." Trans. K. Perrotta.

John Climacus
Quoted in B. Pennington, *Centering Prayer.* New York: Doubleday Image, 1980.

John of the Cross
Dark Night of the Soul. Trans. E. A. Peers.New York: Doubleday Image, 1959.

John Henry Newman
Meditations and Devotions of the Late Cardinal Newman. London: Longmans, Green, 1893.
Parochial and Plain Sermons, VII.

John XXIII
Journal of a Soul. Trans. D. White. New York: McGraw-Hill, 1964.

John Vianney
Little Catechism of the Curé of Ars. Rockford, Ill.: Tan, 1994.
Sermons for the Sundays and Feasts of the Year by the Curé of Ars. New York: Joseph F. Wagner, 1901.

Josemaría Escrivá de Balaguer
The Way. New York, London: Scepter, 1979.

Julian of Norwich
Enfolded in Love: Daily Readings with Julian of Norwich. Ed. R.
Llewelyn. London: Darton, Longmand and Todd, 1980.

Brother Lawrence of the Resurrection
The Practice of the Presence of God. Ed. C. De Meester. Trans.
Salvatore Sciuba. Washington, D.C.: Institute of Carmelite
Studies, 1994.
Walking With the Father. Wisdom From Brother Lawrence. Ed. P.
Mitchell. Ijamsville, Md.: The Word Among Us, 1999.

Louise de Marillac
*Some Counsels of St. Vincent de Paul to which is appended The
Thoughts of Mademoiselle LeGras*. Trans. E.K. Saunders. London:
Heath, Cranton, & Ouseley Ltd. 1914.

Lucien-Louis Bunel (Père Jacques)
Murphy, F. *Père Jacques: Resplendent in Victory*. Washington, D.C.:
ICS, 1998.

Marie of the Incarnation
*The Autobiography of Venerable Marie of the Incarnation, O.S.U.
Mystic and Missionary*. Trans. J. Sullivan.Chicago: Loyola, 1964.
Selected Writings. Ed. I. Mahoney. New York: Paulist, 1989.
Le Témoignage de Marie de l'Incarnation. Ed. A. Jamet. Paris:
Gabriel Beauchesne, 1932.
Jette, F. *The Spiritual Teaching of Mary of the Incarnation*. Trans. M.
M. Herman. New York: Sheed and Ward, 1963.

Mary Euphrasia Pelletier
Bernoville, G. *Saint Mary Euphrasia*. Westminster, Md.: Newman,
1959.

Peter of Alcantara
Treatise on Prayer and Meditation. Trans. D. Devas.Westminster,
   Md.: Newman Press, 1949.

Peter Julian Eymard
Tesnière, A. *St. Peter Julian Eymard, The Priest of the Eucharist*. New
   York: Eymard League, 1962.

Philip Neri
Capocelatro, A. *The Life of Saint Philip Neri*. London: Burns &
   Oates, 1882.
Matthews, V. J. *St. Philip Neri*. Rockford, Ill.: Tan, 1984.
Ponnelle and Bordet. *St. Philip Neri and His Times*. London: Sheed
   & Ward, 1932.
Türks, P. *Philip Neri The Fire of Joy*. New York: Alba, 1995.

Raymond of Capua
The Life of Catherine of Siena. Trans. E. Cartier.Philadelphia: Peter F.
   Cunningham, 1865.
The Life of Catherine of Siena. Trans. C. Kearns.Wilmington, Del.:
   Michael Glazier, 1980.

Solanus Casey
Crosby, M. *Solanus Casey, the Official Account of a Virtuous
   American Life*. New York: Crossroad, 2000.
Odell, C. *Father Solanus*. Huntington, Ind.: Our Sunday Visitor,
   1988.

Teresa of Avila
The Collected Works of St. Teresa of Avila Vol. 2: *The Way of Perfection,
   Meditations on the Song of Songs, Interior Castle*. Trans. K.
   Kavanaugh and O. Rodriguez. Washington, D.C.: ICS, 1980.
The Life of Teresa of Jesus. Trans. E.A. Peers.Garden City, New York:
   Doubleday Image, 1960.
Life of St. Teresa, Written by Herself. Trans. D. Lewis. Westminster,
   Md.: Newman, 1916.

Interior Castle. Trans. E.A. Peers. Garden City, NY: Doubleday Image, 1961.

The Interior Castle or the Mansions. Trans. a Discalced Carmelite. London: Sands, 1945.

The Way of Perfection. Trans. E.A. Peers.Garden City, NY: Doubleday Image, 1964.

The Way of Perfection. Trans. A. Alexander.Cork: Mercier, 1946.

Thérèse of Lisieux

Autobiography. Trans. J. Ryan. New York: Doubleday, 1957.

Thoughts of Saint Therese. Trans. Irish Carmelite. Rockford, Ill.: Tan, 1988.

Thomas Aquinas

The Three Greatest Prayers. Manchester, N.H.: Sophia Institute, 1990.

Thomas à Kempis

The Imitation of Christ. Trans. L. Sherley-Price. New York: Penguin, 1952.

Thomas More

Prayers of St. Thomas More and Treatise on the Holy Eucharist. London: Burns, Oates, & Washbourne, 1938.

The Tower Works: Devotional Writings. Ed. G. Haupt. New Haven and London: Yale, 1980.

Titus Brandsma

Schevers, J. "Titus Brandsma—Carmelite Martyr." *Spiritual Life* 31, no. 4 (winter 1985) 195–206.

Veronica Giuliani

Gaudoin-Parker, M. *A Window on the Mystery of Faith.* New York: Alba, 1997.

Vincent de Paul

Vincent de Paul and Louise de Marillac: Rules, Conferences, and Writings. Ed. F. Ryan and J. Rybolt. New York: Paulist, 1995.

The Conferences of St. Vincent de Paul to the Sisters of Charity. Vols. 1-4. Trans. J. Leonard.Westminster, Md.: Newman Press, 1938.

William of St. Thierry

The Golden Epistle. Trans. T. Berkeley.Spencer, Mass.: Cistercian, 1971.

On Contemplating God. Trans. Sr. Penelope. Spencer, Mass.: Cistercian, 1971.

Collections

Early Fathers from the Philokalia. Ed. and Trans. E. Kadloubovsky and G.E.H. Palmer.London: Faber and Faber, 1954.

Ghezzi, B. *Voices of the Saints: A Year of Readings.* New York: Doubleday, 2000.

Merton, Thomas. *The Wisdom of the Desert.* New York: New Directions, 1970.

Prie dans le secret. Recueil de prières. Ed. R. Claude, and J. Feder. Paris: Casterman, 1966.

A Select Library of the Nicene and Post-Nicene Fathers of the Christian Church. Ed. P. Schaff. Christian Literature, 1887-1894.

Ward, B. *Sayings of the Desert Fathers: The Alphabetical Collection.* Kalamazoo, Mich.: Cistercian, 1975.

Writings from the Philokalia on Prayer of the Heart. Ed. and Trans. E. Kadloubovsky and G.E.H. Palmer.London: Faber and Faber, 1951.